Adventures and Advice
about
Acting in TV Commercials

Adventures and Advice about Acting in TV Commercials

Gwen Horn Willson

VANTAGE PRESS
New York

Published by Vantage Press, Inc.
516 West 34th Street, New York, New York 10001

Manufactured in the United States of America
ISBN: 0-533-10751-2

Library of Congress Catalog Card No.: 93-94056

0 9 8 7 6 5 4 3 2 1

To sons Steve and Brad and their families,
to Dick Barth, agent supreme,
and to actors everywhere whom I have known and loved;
to the above for their continued interest and support—
applause, applause!

Contents

Acknowledgments

To PRODUCER Mel Kane, who started me on this exciting journey.

To AGENTS Sutton, Barth & Vennari, who guided me with great skill.

To CASTING DIRECTORS Baker-Nisbet, Analise Collins, Mick Dowd, Judy Elkins, Barbara and Paul Ely, Danny Goldman, Arlene Glucksman, Barbara Greco, Denny Harris, Dorothy Kelly, Debby Kurtz, Judy Landau, Mike Lien, Beverly Long, Sheila Manning, Jessica Overwise, Shancy Pierce, Phyllis Ricci, Melanie Sherwood, Ava Shevitt, Pam Sparks, Estelle Tepper, and Richard Waterhouse, who sent me on the right path to the directors and sponsors who hired me.

To DIRECTORS Sid Avery, Allen Blake, Jack De Sort, David Farrow, Piers Haggard, Jack Harris, Bill Hudson, Philip Labhart, Brian Lai, Michael Moir, John Orluff, Laura Patterson, Earl Rath, Ray Rivas, Henry Trettin, Deryn Warren, Bill Wertz, Jonathon Yarbrough, and other wonderful directors (whose names I'm sorry I didn't record), for getting the show on the road.

To ACTORS Dana Andrews, Bryan O'Byrne, George Gobel, Alan Hale, Jr., Stacy Keach, Sr., Jack Klugman, Art Linkletter, Frances Reid, Cesar Romero, O. J. Simpson, Don Starr, and Jesse White, who kept the wheels turning.

To FRIENDS Carole Bellmyre, Jeanette O'Connor, Fran and Bill Erwin, Jean and Tom Reeves, Barbara and Jack Woltz, and Carol Conley, who helped me over the bumps along the route, and . . .

To BUSINESSMEN Murray Kalis and Michael Sheldon, who smoothed out the bumps, and . . .

To MY HUSBAND, Bob, who moved, motivated, and literally transported me up that long, long road to fun and fortune.

Introduction

A few can touch the magic string
and noisy fame is proud to win them
Alas for those that never sing
but die with all the music in them.
          —Oliver Wendell Holmes

The Maytag man and I had a rendezvous in Paris. Jack Klugman and I fooled around with Canon Copiers. Stacy Keach, Sr., and I had a second honeymoon on an Amtrak train, and O. J. Simpson and I whizzed around in a Hertz Rent-a-Car. Do I have a way with men? Not really. I get together with neat guys like these when I act in television commercials.

Do you want to make a lot of money in a short time? Do you want to do something you love? Do you want to have fun doing it? If you do, this is the book for you.

So many people have asked me, "How do you get into TV commercials? Where do you start? What do you do?"

I have thought about it for some time and finally decided to write my point of view and what I have seen and done to get into a very remunerative, interesting, and fun business. Yes, it *is* a business—more so than stage work or films, for it is really advertising.

Advertising is the head of our culture at present, and commercials on television have a much bigger influence on people than newspapers, books, or any other form of communication. Creating the words and pictures that will sell a product is the name of the game. Billions of dollars are spent on commercials each year, and the actors in them are the recipients of quite a few of these dollars.

When someone at a party or any group asks, "What do you do?" I never know whether to answer, "I'm an actress," or "I'm in advertising." Since the product is the "star" and I am selling the product, I am, in a way, in advertising.

This is written especially for the beginner, but a few seasoned actors coming to their first commercial interviews are not too sure of their ground and rather uncertain as to what to expect. At least, I have noticed this from their questions. I hope to give the reader an overall picture of all areas of commercial acting and hope that it is helpful.

Statistics change daily, so I'll not attempt to tell you how many television sets are watched worldwide or how many people are watching them, but it is a fact that television keeps growing by leaps and bounds and more and more actors will be needed to fill the ever-increasing demand for performers. Actors make more money in commercials percentage-wise than in films or the stage. Of course, there are the stars who make huge salaries, but I am speaking of the average actor. You can imagine that if you are in a national commercial with perhaps millions of viewers, and you are paid every time it plays over a period of time you will receive a goodly sum. Not only is this good for the pocketbook but for the ego as well.

The Screen Actors Guild has set the minimum wage scale, and a good agent can negotiate for more if it seems feasible.

Living in the Los Angeles area, New York, or Chicago is helpful, but not absolutely necessary. Casting goes on more and more in other cities as time goes on.

Knowing that you will be paid a residual every time the commercial airs is reason enough to be in this business, but the added attraction of exchanging news and views with your peers at interviews, traveling to exciting locations, the challenge of the work itself keeps you going, keeps you young, and keeps you happy.

Well, enough said. Let's get on with it. "Touch the magic string." Sing!

Adventures and Advice
about
Acting in TV Commercials

Part I

Advice

Chapter 1
Desire

One quickly gets readiness in an art where strong desire comes in play.

—Thomas Mann

Let's get right down to the nitty-gritty at the beginning. Face it, unless you have a great desire to do commercial acting, don't try it! Commercial acting is an "iffy" business. You must have the desire to do it, vitality, patience, availability, a thick skin, health, and, of course, talent and craft knowledge; and that's only the beginning.

When I say that you too can do commercials, I mean it, but one must always work diligently for success in any venture one undertakes, and the basis of commercial acting is being able to *act*. Unless you have that foundation you cannot expect the rewards of profit and fun about which I'm writing. Very few people achieve success in this business without working at it. Yes, I know, the performances on commercials look natural and easy, but achieving that naturalness is sometimes more difficult than doing a showy characterization on the stage.

If you are not consumed by this great urge to be an actor and to face every kind of situation as well as lots of rejection, go into another line of work. Only the ambitious and determined survive in this business. I've heard people say, "There's nothing to it; I can do that!" Oh yes, "anybody"

3

may be able to do one or two commercials, but to stay in the business, one must be an actor. Too many situations come up which, unless you can act, you can't handle. Yes, anyone can read a line with intelligence, but it's *how* you read it that makes all the difference. You must have the basics before you start. Get rid of all self-consciousness. You are asked to do many things a self-conscious person would not do.

Take voice lessons, both singing and speaking, take acting classes, read aloud in front of a mirror. Get into little theater plays. Start in a school or church or anyplace that will take you; then, go on to bigger and better productions. Whatever your city has to offer, take advantage of it. There is hardly a town in the United States that doesn't have a facility for putting on a play. Have groups in your own home who are interested in acting, to study lines and scenes together. Many colleges and universities have fine classes in commercial acting, which can be very helpful. I cannot impress upon you enough how much the motto "Be Prepared" means in this business. No matter how much you think you already know, there are always new skills and techniques to learn.

Just to show you how important it is to be an *actor,* one day the handsomest man I'd ever seen was working on a gas line outside my house, so I went out to talk to him about doing commercials. He said he'd love it! So I told him I'd tell my agent about him, being sure the agency would take him. I called my agent and said, "This is the best-looking man in the world!"

He asked, "Is he an actor?"

I said, "Well, no-o-o-o, but he's—"

My agent interrupted. "Unless he's an actor, we can't take him."

So you see, good looks won't make it in commercials unless you have the craft of acting mastered too.

Top commercial agent Dick Barth, in speaking to beginners says, "Work on your acting in classes, workshops, and plays until you have people excited enough about you to call good agents to recommend you."

If you really have a long-range goal for yourself, be careful how you use your time. Having a burning desire to succeed means giving up frivolous extraneous activities. Start small, look ahead to what the future can bring, and then keep at it. This may sound like a very heavy trip for just doing commercials; but when you consider the monetary rewards alone, to say nothing of the excitement and pleasure experienced in the business, it is important to put all your eggs in one basket. Singleness of purpose cannot be underestimated. Put all of your energy into what you want to be and do, picture yourself a success, and little by little, step by step, you'll find you have reached your goal.

I will not belabor these points further. Just remember what I tell you, "Work, study, practice, and you'll get there." It all depends on the strength of your desire. It has been said, "Great people are ordinary people who are determined."

Chapter 2
Getting Your Foot in the Door

He has the deed half done, who has made a beginning.
                              —Horace (65 B.C.)

Okay, let's get started. Are you prepared? Can you face an interview without getting flustered? Have you studied, practiced, and rehearsed? Can you read a short scene with some sense and personality showing?

When you feel you have enough self-confidence to "face the music," have a good eight-by-ten head shot taken by a reputable photographer. It should look like you do when you start seeing agents. Decide the look you want to keep for a while and go for it. In commercials, we're supposed to be real people, not "reel" people. You are safer in commercials not looking too different, as your chances are limited if you do. The person who works a lot has a kind of "middle America face"; I think you know what I mean. You see, if you're not too outstanding looking, you can work in many things where you won't be recognized immediately and seem more like just a man or woman on the bus, on the street, etc. On the other side of the coin, if you have an outstanding feature, e.g., large nose, too fat, too short, too thin, once in a while that may be just the distinguishing feature the sponsor needs to sell his product, and people may begin to know and love you because of it. In recent years, it has become more and more popular to use many different ethnic groups. So, if you feel you may be overlooked because you are a minority, don't let that stop you. Producers and sponsors are hiring all races and the disabled to make their commercials more interesting and fair to everyone.

After having your picture taken, have a batch of eight-by-ten glossies made from the best print. Then get a list of reputable commercial agents from a friend in the business or call or write the Screen Actors Guild and ask for a list. Then write a short resumé of your background, even if you've done only school plays, including drama classes you have taken, etc. Send this and the photograph, with a short letter asking for an interview, to several agents. Wait until you are sure they have received them and then call each one. Say something like this, "Hi, I'm George Brown. I sent you a picture and resumé, and I was wondering if I could come in and see 'Mr. Agent' for a few moments?" They will either say yes or no. If they say yes, you know they like your look; if no, go on to the next agent. Most people get a lot of rejection at first, but one does get used to it. Just keep at it. Go down the list until somebody will see you. Be diligent, and somehow, somewhere, some-time, some agent will say, "Yes, you're just what we're looking for." If this doesn't work, there are other ways. Keep at it. Get into plays. An agent may see you and pick you up from that. Perhaps a friend knows an agent who will take you. Anyway, "Where there's a will, there's a way."

Even if you start with a lesser known agent, you are getting your feet wet. He/she will send you on fewer calls than the larger, more well-known agent, but at least you are getting the feel of the business. After going on several interviews, you will gain more confidence and learn by doing. Agents do make all the difference in the world though. For five or six years, I was with a mediocre commercial agent who got me more print work (pictures in magazines, etc.) than commercials. I thought my age was holding me back. It wasn't my age: it was my "age-nt." Finally, I met an influential man from a large advertising agency who recommended me to the fine agents I now have, and the difference was like night and day. All of a sudden, I was going out on interviews constantly and getting one commercial job after another. So the agent you have makes all the difference in the world. You are the same person, but a good agent can change you from a "so-so" productive commercial actor to a real money-maker!

Read *The NY Agent Book,* 1987, by K. Callan and *The LA Agent Book,* 1988, by the same author.

One of the most important tools of the trade is the composite, which consists of several different types of pictures and poses on one page. One should be given to the casting director at each interview. After an agent has agreed to represent you, he/she will tell you what kind of composites to have made. Do not do this beforehand, as they are expensive. Some commercial agents want pictures only and some want pictures with a resumé added. I have included some composites of working actors in this book so you can get an idea of the various types in use.

Another tool for the actor is an outside answering service or an answering machine in your home. All agents require this, otherwise you will miss many important calls and job opportunities.

Also, if you are job-seeking in California, be sure to have a *Thomas Guide* to help you get to your desired interview destination and job location. This book is almost a must in getting you to the right place at the right time. I recommend you have these things to aid you in your career hunt.

ESTHER SPENCER

This is a second career for Esther, who is a thirty-three year veteran of the Los Angeles County Sheriff's Department. After having studies acting recently, and appearing in little theater and college plays, agents realized her potential and signed her. This should give mature newcomers hope. (Sutton, Barth, & Vennari Talent Agents, 145 South Fairfax Avenue, Los Angeles, CA 90036)

Chapter 3
Interviews

Be like the turtle; he doesn't get anyplace unless he sticks his neck out.

—Anon.

You are going on your first interview. Your agent calls and says, "Alice, you have an interview tomorrow at 3:00 P.M." Then he gives you a specific address and says, "You are a thirtyish mother. Wear a house dress. This is for a breakfast cereal. See Judy."

You plan ahead. You get your wardrobe prepared and decide on the proper hairdo and makeup. Have everything ready beforehand, so you will not be rushed at the last minute. Try to get there twenty minutes ahead of time so you'll have time to look over the copy. When you arrive at the appointment place, the first thing to do is look for the "sign-in sheet" and sign it. This has several columns for you to fill in, e.g., name, social security number, agent, appointment, time of arrival, etc. Also, if there's a storyboard (pictures of the scene) available, study it carefully so that you'll know how they want the scene to look. Then look for the copy (script); it should be on the same table. If not, ask one of the other actors there or the casting director if there is copy for you to read. Look it over. If there is quite a bit of dialogue, go to a quiet corner and study it until you know the gist of it. Do not, and I repeat, *do not,* sit and chat with other actors around you unless you are a very seasoned performer. There are a few actors around who have been doing commercials for years and would love to keep you occupied so you won't be able to study and concentrate. I have seen too many people chatting animatedly with fellow actors, and when they go in for the interview, they haven't the vaguest notion of what they are supposed to be doing or the character they are supposed to portray. It looks easy, only a few lines—nothing to it. Don't be too sure. Remember, there may be twenty-five other people after the same job. There's that extra, little, clever something you thought of to do that might get it for you. When they call your name, *you* will know what you're doing, and those who have been "running off at the mouth" won't.

This is a true story. I was called to a production company to read for a part with an actor who was to play my husband. I had no idea who the man might be. When I arrived at the designated place and picked up the copy, I glanced around the room for an actor to rehearse the lines with me for those two parts. There were at least fifty actors and actresses there waiting their turn. I found a place to sit next to an actor I had never seen. I said to him, "Hi, would you mind going over lines with me?"

He gave me a disdainful look and said, "I never rehearse."

I said, "Well, you don't have to rehearse yourself, but would you mind just reading the cues so that *I* can rehearse?"

He repeated, "I never rehearse."

I couldn't believe my ears. Most actors are so happy to have someone with whom to practice that they jump at the chance, and most actors are helpful. After all, he and I weren't in competition. I didn't say another word, but I got up, found a corner by myself, and started studying the lines.

It is true that some experienced actors prefer not to rehearse because they feel they can be more effective with a spontaneous reading, but I think that knowing the copy is more important. That way you can relax and let your personality come through rather than nervously searching for the next line. This is especially true in commercials where the copy has to be adhered to exactly as written.

In a few moments, an actor walked in who had done a commercial with me previously. I said to him, "Hi, Wayne, let's go someplace and rehearse." So the two of us went into a dressing room and went over the little scene about ten times. Then we went back and waited. As we were waiting, the actor who wouldn't rehearse walked by with another actress on his way to the interview room. As he walked by, he looked at me and said, "See, you weren't going to be my partner anyway!"

Again, I couldn't believe my ears. Well, as it turned out, Wayne and I both got the job! We knew what we were doing. Though I don't have much revenge in my soul, if I ever see that actor again, I swear I'm going to say to him, "Well, we got the job because we REHEARSED!"

Before I go on to another subject, I want to emphasize that usually there is plenty of competition. Sometimes there are as many as twenty-five to thirty actors up for the same part. You have to learn to "go with the flow," as they say. After all, only one person will get the part, so do your best and learn to cope.

Okay, let's get on to the interview itself. On the first interview, there will be perhaps only one or two people in the inner office; the casting director and the camera person. Sometimes it may be the director, one is never sure. The first thing they ask you to do is to "slate." I actually didn't know about it on my first interview, and the director said, "Slate, please."

I just stood there on my mark, looking quizzical. Then he said, "Give me your name and agent."

"Oh," I said to myself, "so that's what slate is!"

When they are actually shooting a commercial, they have a slate-board, which you have seen used in making films but not on interviews.

Never tell the casting directors your weaknesses; show them your strengths. Don't say, "Oh, I'm really too old/young for this part" or "I have on the wrong kind of slacks for this" or some other negative statement. Show them how *well* you can do the part, and they won't notice any weaknesses. Communicate confidence, professionalism, even if you don't feel it, and give them a good strong reading. *Never* communicate *fear!* Never comment on how good or bad the copy is. Read it verbatim exactly the way it is written. Hold the copy so that they can see your face. Go there prepared to perform. If you make a mistake, don't stop and apologize—keep right on reading. Act like you know what you're doing.

You should be gracious but not too talkative on interviews. From hard experience I have learned not to talk too much to the interviewer. Be pleasant, smile a lot, but don't try to be clever or make cute remarks. Early on, thinking I was going to be complimentary, I said to the casting director, "I heard that casting directors in Hollywood are so much nicer to actors than casting directors are in New York" (which I had just read someplace).

This casting director said, "I just flew in from New York last night!"

Flustered, I mumbled something inane, trying to cover up my "boo-boo"—only making it worse.

Did I get the job? Nope! I could have been the greatest

actress on earth and they wouldn't have hired me. Let me tell you something; they have to *like* you. Sometimes they will hire a lesser actor because he or she is personable and easy to get along with. If there's anything they *don't* like, it's a complainer, an egotist, an argumentative type, or one with other unbecoming characteristics. So be pleasant, cooperative, and a wee bit humble.

I don't mean overdo it, but *do* let the director be boss, do exactly as he or she says, and you'll get along fine. Sometimes he/she will have you do the same scene several times in various ways. This usually means they like you and see something interesting about you. When you are finished, exit gracefully with a "thank you." There are some commercial actors who get quite friendly with casting directors and really carry on with hugs, kisses, and conversation. This is all right if you have seen them often enough to know them well; otherwise, keep the repartee to a minimum.

There are various types of interviews. Sometimes you may just talk one to one with the casting director, but most of the time, they will put the scene or speech on video tape. Other times you may do the scene with no tape at all, and they make their decision with just the interview and your photograph. Very seldom do you hold the copy; there is usually a large cue card near the camera and you read from that. Even this takes practice, and most actors don't like this way of reading, but that's the way it is.

If and when you get a "call-back," there will be many more people in the interview room, i.e. sponsors, advertising people, producers, director, wardrobe people, etc. This is when they separate the winners from the losers. "Many are called but few are chosen" in this business, so don't beat yourself all the way home saying, "Why didn't I do it *this* way, or *that* way," . . . or "Why didn't I wear something different," etc., etc. Forget it and go on to tomorrow. There's always another interview and commercial coming up, so look forward to that. Just do your best each time and be optimistic. I've been to over forty production companies in the past few years, many of them several times, and there are always new ones popping up—so, if one doesn't hire you, perhaps the next one will. Comes the day your agent calls and says, "You got the job!" Hallelujah! Raise the flag and celebrate!

Chapter 4
Wardrobe

Clothes make the man (and woman).

—Anon.

The first call you get following the one from your agent, is from wardrobe, and they set a time for your wardrobe call, which is usually in the next day or two. The wardrobe person asks you to bring all of the wardrobe you have that fits the scene and character you're playing. They decide at that time what they can use of yours and what has to be purchased. The wardrobe person (usually a girl) buys whatever you cannot furnish and brings it to the "shoot." There is always time for her to press or hem any of it if that needs doing (by the way, most of the time they will let you purchase at half-price any of the items you have worn) once the "shoot" is finished.

Following is a list of the clothing I have taken on an actual wardrobe call:

5 blouses	4 pairs of shoes
2 blazers	3 purses
3 hats	3 sweaters
3 dresses	2 skirts

This may seem like a lot of packing to do for a wardrobe call, but it is a joint effort, and we all want it right.

There may be a wardrobe call where the girl says, "Just bring a couple of blouses and skirts in monotone colors," or to a man, "A couple of plaid shirts and two pairs of slacks should do it." So, it depends on the wardrobe person and the commercial itself. I will say though, that they are usually very particular about every item of clothing to be worn. Actually, sometimes your wardrobe can help sway them to hire you. I was sent on an interview for a photo company, and the scene was a birthday party where pictures were being taken.

On the first call, I wore a nice dress, but not the perfect dress. When I got a "call-back" for the second interview, I went shopping the afternoon before and bought a beautiful, dressy birthday-party type dress. I felt the expense was worth the gamble. Well, when I walked into the outer office and looked at the other "call-back" ladies, I was sure I had it in the bag. Some of them had on drab looking dresses, suits, etc., none of which looked like a birthday party. Of course, I had my hair done accordingly. I felt good and confident, and I'm sure this reflected on the casting people, for I did get the commercial. I am sure that if I had worn a drab, uninteresting outfit, I might not have been cast.

In most cases though, it is a good idea to wear the same outfit to the call-back that you wore to the initial interview: the wardrobe may have added to their interest in you. I was told by a casting director that the director had said, "Get me the gal in the green sweater." Well, they didn't use the green sweater in the commercial, but it was bright enough to identify me. "Never leave a stone unturned" in this business. Go to each interview as if it were the only one. Approach each one with concentration and enthusiasm, because every facet, i.e., looks, personality, wardrobe, hair, and talent are all considered.

17

Once I had two wardrobe calls at exactly the same time—9:00 A.M. in the morning. My agent could have handled the situation for me; but one of the calls came late in the evening, so I had to handle it myself. I thought over both commercials. Both were national, both large, well-known companies, but one was a year 'round product and the other seasonal. Also, the location for the year 'round product was closer to my home, so I decided to go to it first. I called the other production company and told them I was sorry but that I would be about an hour late. I try never to be late or miss an appointment, but there was no way out of this one. They weren't very nice about it on the phone, for which I couldn't blame them.

The first wardrobe call took forever and I almost got sick from nerves trying to get away from there. After getting back into my street clothes to leave, they remembered that they had forgotten to take a Polaroid of me in my wardrobe, so I had to put it all back on again. I was fit to be tied, but of course, I kept smiling. Well, I finally got out of there and dashed twenty miles over one of the canyon roads to the other call. You can imagine how much stuff I had in my car for two *entirely* different types of wardrobe. Believe it or not, when I got to the other call (two hours late), they were charming to me, calm as cucumbers, relaxed, and said, "Hi, Gwen, sit down and have a cup of coffee." Whew! Of course, you may not always be so lucky.

Even so, these are the hazards of the business that can give you a lot of stress. I suggest some form of daily relaxation—meditation, aerobics, walking, running—whatever turns you *off* to get rid of the tension.

I want to make this very clear. You do not *have* to buy anything at all, especially if you are new in the business.

Take what you have, and if it isn't just right, they will furnish it.

Though the clothes are important, you got the job because you are YOU!

Chapter 5

Improvisation and Cold Reading

There is nothing which persevering effort and unceasing diligent care cannot overcome.

—Seneca

Improvisation is a *must* in commercial acting. You are asked to do a scene at a moment's notice, and do it convincingly. There is no time for study when it comes to improvisation, for you are asked to do it *now*.

When you go to an interview and look at the storyboard, you will see several pictures depicting the scene required by the commercial. If there is no dialogue, it will be necessary for you to draw on your own imagination and pantomime skills to put the scene across. The director will describe the scene to you, and you are expected to act it out immediately. Quick thinking is required in commercial acting, as you must quickly dream up a more clever way to do the scene than the other actors. Of course, you never get to watch the others, so you're not sure what they are doing. This means you must try harder. If the director says, "Now, Larry, I want you to take a drink of the beverage and react in an affectionate way towards Elaine." Okay, that sounds easy enough, but wait—every other actor gets the same direction. So it is up to you to think of a special something to add to it, i.e., pinching her

20

cheek, throwing her a kiss, winking, or whatever comes to mind that will make you stand out from the others. Whatever you decide to do, it should be a natural reaction utilizing your own special personality traits. You want them to remember you, and they will not remember an actor who is boring or humdrum.

Have you ever played charades? Well, it's similar to that. You are given a specific subject, and you get up and act it out. As a matter of fact, playing charades with family or friends is a good way to practice doing commercial improvisation. If you act out various charades often enough, you will soon become very adept at improvising. In addition, the more you perform in front of people, the more confidence you will gain.

If you want to take it further, join a class in improvisation. There are classes branching out all over for every phase of the business, and this is just one of them. In this way, you can watch your peers and listen to critiques of your work and theirs; consequently, doing "improvs" will soon become second nature to you. Many classes will tape students doing commercials and with this, you can watch yourself and catch mistakes and unattractive mannerisms. One student said while watching herself on a tape in class, she saw her eyes were blinking too much. She worked on this, and the next week in class watched herself again and found she had corrected this problem. It is amazing what just watching yourself can do to help improve your improvisational skills.

Imagination is all-important in improvisation. Mickey Rooney says actors should rely on their complete individuality.

Cold Reading

When you read the copy for the casting director or director for the first time at an interview, it is called a cold reading. The powers that be expect you to be able to read the copy clearly, and with a maximum amount of vitality. What you are reading in a commercial covers the span of only a few seconds, so you must give it all the personality you can. It is quite different from doing a scene in a play, where much more time is allowed to get an idea across. In a commercial you have to get it across immediately. Too, you must realize there is usually an instantaneous change of ideas in a commercial. For instance, a man at a dinner party says regretfully that he cannot have any dessert because he is watching his weight. Then *presto,* the hostess says, "Oh, but this is Clark's sugar-free sherbet, made especially for people on a diet!" He tastes it, smiles, and says, "Ummm, this is delicious—better than ice cream!" This premise occurs in a great many commercials—the negative thought and lines followed by the quick change-over to the positive. The actors must be sure to convey this idea immediately to get the effect the sponsor wants, to sell the product. First the obstacle, then the objective. The conflict makes it happen.

For a good cold reading, you should have the eye of the director. Look at yourself through his/her eye. What would he/she see in you? If the copy has quite a bit of dialogue, pick out the part you think you can do best, slow down, and stop for a moment—then go on and make it your *best* moment!

Just before you read, decide on a physical gesture you can incorporate in the scene, give the body something to do—something simple, like clasping your hands, pushing back a strand of hair, fixing a tie or scarf, etc. Any movement to make the reading more interesting and eye-catching.

As I have mentioned previously, try to get to the interview fifteen or twenty minutes prior to your appointment time and study the scene thoroughly. You needn't memorize it all, but it helps to have the first and last lines memorized. That way, you can catch their attention immediately and leave them with a positive attitude towards you. Every school and coach emphasizes this.

Cue Cards

There are usually cue cards near the camera, so with practice, you can learn to glance quickly at the lines and then toward the camera or the other actor without too much hesitation. This all takes practice, but it comes in time.

If the copy is long, there's a knack to reading cue cards, which helps you look as though you are not reading. Of course, you must read the words several times before you go into the audition room, so that you have the gist of the copy. Then, as I mentioned before, try to have the first line memorized. After you say that line, look at the next one and quickly read ahead mentally, so when you are verbalizing it, you are not looking at the cue card. When you have to glance at the card again, pause momentarily (as if musing) and digest the next sentence the same way. If you are reading it in a conversational manner, it will seem perfectly natural for you to pause as if searching for the correct word, just as you would in a normal conversation. You might turn your head a bit and laugh or sigh (depending on the copy), utilizing a chance to take a look at the cue card before turning back to the camera.

If there are directions in the script that indicate a physical movement, indicate a partial movement of the body—you needn't go all the way with it, but do indicate it.

If there's a prop or the product to be held, and they don't give you something to hold, pantomime it. It is better than standing there doing nothing.

If you are reading with another person, *listen* to what he or she is saying and react accordingly. *Listening* is extremely important in *any* form of acting.

Don't hurry! This is your moment. Take the time to do it right. After you have the job, and have it all memorized—*then* you can time it according to the dictates of the commercial.

Concentrate on the reading! Forget that you got a traffic ticket this morning or that you have a headache—leave all the stress outside the door. This is what you are doing *now*. This is the most important thing to do right at this moment, and you want to do it right! Right? After all, this one job could pay your rent and car payments, so give it all you've got.

Producer Stephen J. Cannell says "A cold reading should actually be a performance." Pretend this is the end result. Don't say to yourself, "Well, this is just a reading, and I'll improve on it with time." You can't *do* that. The director isn't going to wait for the next time. You have to give it your best shot at the beginning. This is not a play that you'll be honing and rehearsing for weeks: this is thirty to sixty seconds of acting that you have to sell immediately!

The best thing to do for practice is to read any and everything you can get your hands on. Pick up some advertising copy in a magazine, sit in front of a mirror, and read fresh copy every day. You will see how soon you'll find your eyes looking at yourself instead of buried in the reading material. That's the way they want it. They want to see your face as much as possible. Remember, everything becomes easier with effort and care.

*   *   *

Practice reading these commercials aloud:

Young woman: I'm a working girl, and you know what that means—long hours, and very little time to cook. I can't *tell* you how I look forward to coming home at night, slipping into something comfortable, and popping a TENDER SLENDER dinner into the microwave. No muss, no fuss, and so many choices—shrimp, chicken, pasta, you name it—and so low in calories!

I've got my TV set and my TENDER SLENDER dinner! Who needs a date?

*   *   *

Young man: Some guys think they should look really macho with stubble on their faces and smelling like a stevedore to attract girls. Not me! I like to look like I just had a shower and shave, but most of all, I like to smell goo-ood!

When I meet a girl, I want her to say, "Ooh-ooh, what is that stuff you've got on?" And I say, "That's FRENCH TABOO after shave," and then she grabs me and kisses me—oops, I'm dreaming! But it could happen, right?

Voice-over (*Woman's voice low and sexy*): FRENCH TABOO cologne and after shave. Ooh, ooh good!

Chapter 6
Actual Work Days

There is a difference between wishing and dreaming and actually doing.

—Anon.

Let me give you an example of an actual work day. The call was for 7:00 A.M. at a production company in the San Fernando Valley. This was for a breakfast cereal. When I arrived, other actors were there waiting for a van to take us to a farm in Santa Paula for the "shoot." Around 8:30 we were organized and took off in the van for the fifty-mile trip.

There were four actors, a make-up man, and a wardrobe girl as passengers. There's a great deal of camaraderie on a commercial job, and we surely enjoyed the trip. We arrived at an old-fashioned farmhouse in the country, and the trucks with equipment and crew were already there. There were all kinds of things to eat and drink outside on a long table for anyone who was hungry or thirsty. It surely is easy to gain weight on a working day if one isn't careful. Before doing anything, however, you find your assigned motor home dressing room and check with the wardrobe person to see if there are any changes in costume. Following that, you check with the make-up person so that you will be available when your turn comes. After you are all dressed and made up, you wait for them

26

to call you. It's said that half your time in show business is made up of waiting—that holds true in commercials.

This was a very homey husband-and-wife scene in the kitchen of a farmhouse. It was a very small room and quite warm. There were at least twelve people squeezed in there, plus the camera, lights, and other equipment, to say nothing of a large tuba that the farmer was to play. We were all hot and perspiring before it was over.

Sometimes the director and the sponsor don't agree and each will give you different directions. This happened to us, and we were trying to please both. One must really figure out who is in charge. It usually is the director, but the sponsor has a preconceived idea of how he wants his product presented, and that must be considered. Since the sponsor pays the bills, it is important to listen to him. Finally, the director and the sponsor came to a meeting of the minds, and we got along fine.

I must have poured milk on forty successive bowls of cereal in the morning. The property people kept handing me fresh bowls of cereal and strawberries for each "take." We had a little ditty to sing too, which had to be repeated that many times also. After singing and pouring all morning, we still hadn't finished at lunchtime.

A catering service from Los Angeles brought us a wonderful lunch, which some people ate at a long table they provided, while others sat on the old-fashioned porch steps and rocking chairs. It felt like we were going back in time. The fact that fried chicken and watermelon were on the menu added to that old country feeling.

After lunch, we had our make-up freshened and started shooting again. Most of the "takes" this time were close-ups on our faces, and also on our hands handling the product. When they finally finished doing our scene, they moved to a field nearby to shoot a scene for another commercial for the same product, using the other actors who had come with us in the van. We waited quite some time until they completed their scene so that all of us could return in the same van. We were much quieter on the way home, like returning from a holiday, all of us pleasantly relaxed after a satisfying day.

There are contracts to sign during the day and W-4 forms to complete, plus sign-in and sign-out sheets. All this, as well as pay and any overtime, are verified by the Screen Actors Guild.

Incidentally, the short musical phrase we sang had been recorded the night before at A & M Records in Hollywood. A top musical director played the piano for us. That was fun too, and very good pay. A & M Records is where many of the young rock stars record. As one of them passed in the hall carrying his guitar, I almost expected him to say, "What's a nice little lady like you doing in a place like this?"

*   *   *

Every "shoot" is different of course. Another example would be a bug spray commercial that aired in the Southern states and Hawaii. We started shooting at *12:30 Friday afternoon* and worked straight through until *6:30 Saturday morning*. We had a twelve-hour break after that, so I went home and rested. Then I drove back and began again at 6:30 P.M. Saturday, finishing at 4:30 A.M. Sunday. Of course we had breaks for lunch, dinner, and whatever else union rules required.

As I recall, it was 2:00 A.M. Saturday morning when the assistant director told me it was time for my dinner break. I asked, "Is anyone else going on a dinner break?" He said, "No, just you." Since I was the only actor on the set with about thirty other people working on the project, I felt ridiculous taking time off for dinner, so I skipped it. However, those *are* union rules. Anyway, there's always so much food around that it's no sacrifice to go without dinner at 2:00 A.M. Actually, when you're inside a sound stage for eighteen hours straight, it's hard to tell which meal is next.

The reason this thirty-second commercial took so long to shoot was because of the exploding bugs they used. They had huge bugs on wires swirling around my head. They were at least twelve inches long and were made of light-weight plastic, I believe. A man stood on a catwalk above me controlling them. It took a long time to get the right level since the bugs kept hitting me on the head, which really didn't hurt. When they got this technicality corrected, we rehearsed all the action of me ducking and spraying them with the bug spray. I was portraying a housewife sitting in a rocker on her front porch and showing all her reactions to these huge insects buzzing about. Every time I sprayed one, the bug would literally explode. The technical crew actually exploded them with gunpowder behind a glass enclosure, with a bright flash lighting up each explosion. This was done at a different time than my action shots.

Later they had to match the shots of me spraying the bugs and the explosions. This was an extremely difficult shoot and the technical crew deserved a medal. It took twenty-eight hours, but the rewards were great! It turned out to be an extremely funny and popular commercial; and the double and triple time payments for Saturday and Sunday were not bad, not bad at all!

Driving home through Hollywood at 5:00 A.M. on Sunday morning is an eerie experience: I have never seen the town so quiet, innocent, and clean-looking. I think that is why I love this work so much—there are so many new experiences daily that one can never tire of it.

*   *   *

A few years ago, a well-known film director from England came to California with his crew to shoot a commercial for a worldwide children's product. They came here to take advantage of our *wonderful* weather! I was hired to play the English nanny. It was an outside shoot in an area resembling the English countryside. It was a freezing day in February and all of us Americans were shivering, while those young Englishmen were doing their work in shorts and bathing trunks. I thought they were crazy and told them so. I believe they assumed that we dress that way all year 'round in "sunny" California.

We worked very hard most of the day before it started to drizzle—then the drizzle became a downpour. There was no way we could finish the project, so we were called back for the next day. Originally, it was to have been a one-day shoot.

Now, this commercial paid $750 per day (more than twice the minimum daily scale at the time), because there would be no residuals coming from England. Just before going home, they handed $750 in cash from a large metal cash box to all the actors. It struck me as funny because I'd never been paid that way. But, hey—cash is every bit as good as a check—isn't it?

The problem was that the little boy in the scenes with me had a different job the next day, so they had to quickly hire another boy and start from scratch the following morning.

It was still drizzly and even chillier the next A.M., but clear enough to work. Those English fellows were still running around in their swim trunks. It reminded me of many tourists who come to Hollywood in mid-winter wearing Hawaiian shirts and muumuus—just because it's California, regardless of the weather. Anyway, the rest of us were shivering in our boots.

When we finally finished, we queued up in line again to collect our $750 daily dole, which was okay by me. The whole thing was fun, interesting, different, and those Englishmen never did put on even a T-shirt. Well, southern California *is* southern California, right? I smile when I recall that one.

The saying, "Mad dogs and Englishmen go out in the noonday sun" is one thing, but how about wearing bathing suits in 36 degree temperature? Wonderful California weather? Bet they were glad to get back to England. Hail Britannia! And God save the Queen!

Chapter 7
Availability

There is a tide in the affairs of men, which, taken at the flood, leads on to fortune: omitted, all the voyage of their life is bound in shallows and in miseries.
—Shakespeare, *Julius Caesar*

Do not relax if you have a few commercials under your belt, thinking you're going to be on easy street. You must be available every weekday, because you never know when they're going to call you. It is usually the day before the interview. If you have to support yourself until you get commercial jobs, find a nighttime job, a weekend job, or one where there is leeway for you to go on interviews. At first, you will probably not go out so often, so it won't be such a problem; but as time goes on and you get busier, you should be available all day five days a week.

I mean *available*! The agent doesn't ask *you* when you're available. He calls and says something like this: "Joan, you have an interview tomorrow at 11:00 A.M. at such-and-such production company on Melrose Avenue at such-and-such an address. Dress casually. You are to be a mother at a picnic. See Lorraine." That's it. You don't argue. You don't say, "How about two o'clock instead?" You go. The only excuse for not going is illness, an unbreakable doctor's appointment, or perhaps an earthquake. You either do it or you don't. If you really want to make it in commercials, you go to every interview you can. Be grateful they are sending you; there are hundreds of actors who would love to be in your shoes. Take advantage of it and go, go, go!

Here is an example. Business had been slow, and I had no interviews scheduled for a particular Monday, so my husband and I decided to drive from Los Angeles to Santa Barbara to spend a few days. When we arrived, I called my answering service. They said, "Call your agent immediately." When I called him, he said, "You have an interview at 2:30 P.M. today." It was 11:30 A.M. at the time. I said, "I'm in Santa Barbara," and he said, "Well, get down here fast!" Did I say, "No, I can't make it? I don't feel well? We just got here? Sorry, I don't want to come down?" No, I said, "Okay." So-o-o-o, we drove back to L.A.—eighty miles—I ran into my house, fixed my hair, changed clothes, and walked in on the appointment on the dot at 2:30 P.M.! I got the job!

This was really a fun shoot. It was a car commercial and six actors were involved—two teens, two "thirtysomethings," and two "fiftysomethings." On the first day, we were to be packing the car with boxes to demonstrate how large the trunk was, followed by a ride in the car. This was to be finished that day.

We met in the morning in a beautiful park in San Marino. We sat around for a while and got acquainted, then we took short walks while waiting for the crew to get everything set up. One girl even brought her dog along. By lunchtime nothing had been accomplished, so they brought in some delicious food, and we had a picnic in the park—and waited some more. On a cold sound stage, this would have been a bore, but in this gorgeous park, it seemed like a holiday.

Only the gods know what went wrong, but the cameraman never got around to shooting *anything*—so we went home around 5:00 P.M. For that we were each paid $333.25. The next day, they did get around to shooting us packing the trunk, and then they waited for a perfect sunset to photograph us driving away in the car. Well, the perfect sunset never arrived, so we went home. This too paid $333.25. This was to have been a two-day job, but we were all called back on the third day. By this time, we were old friends, had brought books to read, cards to play, jogging shoes, etc. Lunchtime got to be a gala occasion, and the weather kept right on being perfect. Other regular walkers and joggers in the park began stopping by for a visit. It was a kick!

They kept calling us in early, because they were searching for the perfect sunlight to show off the car. Well, another day went by—no heavenly sunrise—no radiant sunset, so guess what? We went home. Another day, another dollar, $333.25 to be exact. The fourth day—the same thing—nothing accomplished, but another $333.25. On the fifth day, same time, same place—again nil, nada, mucho dinero, another $333.25.

By that time, the weekend was upon us. Monday? Back again. At this point, we had fallen in love with the park, one couple had fallen in love with each other, and I had fallen in love with al fresco lunches and the good life.

All of a sudden, there was a rush of activity; they had found their light! Voila!! We hopped in the car, waving out the windows, and *finally* got the perfect shot. What? It's not over? No! Another $333.25 is waiting. We were called back to the studio on Tuesday for some inside shots. The problem was that I had a shoot for a cookie commercial that day way out in the country. What to do? After much phoning back and forth, the A.D.'s (assistant directors) on both sides worked it out so that I could go to the shoot in the country an hour earlier than planned and the shoot in town an hour later. Since they hadn't anticipated the car commercial to last so many days, my agent had already booked me for the second one. They were very nice to work it out that way, and I was grateful to them for that. So there you go—$333.25 for the first commercial, and another $333.25 for the second one on the same day!

At last the car commercial was finished—but believe it or don't—the cookie people called me back for the second day—another $333.25. Now, that's $2,666 for eight days work, but that's only the beginning! After that the residuals started rolling in—over and over again. I'll not make this long story any longer, but I do want you to see how being available gets your bread well buttered. If I hadn't rushed down from Santa Barbara to that interview, I would have missed out on thousands of dollars and a lot of fun too.

The pay scale has risen since that time, as you will see in a later chapter. Also, you may have an agent who can negotiate more than scale for you, so it isn't written in stone that you get just that amount.

Please do not compare this to the salaries of stars or top models. We are speaking here of the average working actor. These examples happened early on to me, and I was thrilled to be getting what I was getting—still am. I'm sure most actors would feel the same.

*   *   *

Do you want to hear about *really* being available? I was taking a week off to be "Back Home Again in Indiana" (as the song goes), to attend my high school class reunion. I was to give a short, humorous talk about commercial acting as part of the program and had previously informed my agent that I would not be available for work that week, so that they would not make any appointments for me. The week prior to my departure, I had been on several interviews. If they really like you, they give you a "call-back" (one more interview) before you are cast in the commercial. I felt safe, knowing that if I got a "call-back," I would ask when it was shooting and could tell them whether I would be available. Well, it so happened—*this one time* I got the job *without* a "call-back." It was to shoot the following Wednesday with a wardrobe call on Tuesday A.M.

It would have been difficult to refuse the job because there were agents, sponsors, and the ad agency involved, so I started the wheels turning to make myself available. Instead of a week in Fort Wayne, I had just thirty-six hours there. It was Friday evening when the news came and since I was leaving that night by plane, I had quite a bit of telephoning to do to rearrange things. Well, I got to the Saturday-night reunion, gave my humorous talk, and had a wonderful time! My friends moved a Thursday night open-house forward to Sunday afternoon for me, and I arrived back in L.A. on Monday. That's about a five-thousand mile round trip just to make a thirty-second commercial. My point, of course, is to show you that making yourself available at all times is how you make your money. You may go to ten interviews and not even get a call-back, but if you happen to miss the eleventh, that may be just the one you would have gotten. So go, go, go!

Chapter 8
Flexibility

The rules of finding success are many and varied, but none of them works unless you do.

—Anon.

Be flexible, change your plans, and hang loose, so to speak. One does make luncheon plans once in a while, and in other businesses, you may possibly make them every day of the week; but it *is* difficult in a business where you never know where you'll be or what you'll be doing on any particular time. There are many people who couldn't hack this unknown, unscheduled existence. That's why there are teachers, office managers, bankers, etc. You couldn't *pay* some people any amount of money for this kind of life, but if you love the business, you'll put up with the odd hours. It's the element of surprise that keeps many creative people going.

Here are some true examples. I planned ahead to go to a celebrity luncheon auction at the famous Beverly Wilshire Hotel. It was a charity benefit for the Motion Picture House and Hospital in Woodland Hills. The tickets were very expensive, and my husband was going too. As I was dressing around 10:30 A.M. (after not having received any interview calls for a week), the phone rang. This is the truth:

My agent: Could you be at such-and-such casting office at 1:00 P.M. dressed in a bathing suit?

Me (*to myself*): Tell me it isn't true!

Me: Could I go a little bit late?

My agent: Nope, they'll be finishing the interviews around that time.

What to do? Well, I quickly collected my bathing suit, terry robe, sandals, and beach hat. Then I finished dressing for the luncheon. I mumbled to myself quite a bit while dressing, trying to figure the logistics. "If I wear my knit suit with the blouse," I thought, "I can change in the ladies room at the hotel and wear the jacket and skirt over the bathing suit to get to the car."

Why didn't I just give up the luncheon? That luncheon cost eighty dollars for two tickets, (most of which went to the hospital), and I meant to *eat* it! Thank goodness it started at twelve, so if they were on time, I might at least get through the main course. We arrived during the social hour, and I went into the ladies room, tipped the attendant, and discussed the possibility of my changing clothes there later. She was very helpful.

They did serve the luncheon fairly close to noon, and I kept saying, sotto voce, "Come on, you waiters, get it on, get it on!" It was kind of interesting to see if I could gracefully eat fast enough to beat the clock. The others at my table were fascinated by my efforts. At about a quarter to one, my husband said, "You've got fifteen minutes to change clothes and drive eight miles."

Oh, boy! I jumped up and said to my table partners kiddingly, "Save my dessert for me!" I raced to the ladies room, took my swim suit out of the bag I was carrying, changed into it, put my skirt and jacket back on, and with my blouse under my arm, I ran through the very proper sophisticated lobby and out the door, where my husband had the car waiting. As we drove through Beverly Hills, (me in the back seat), I slipped off my jacket, donned my terry robe, took off my skirt and shoes and put on my sandals and beach hat. Voila!

I arrived just twelve minutes late for the interview, but there were still several people ahead of me in a variety of beach attire, so-o-o, I was not late for my turn. Usually, *take note,* I am a *half-hour early* for interviews, so don't be late if you can help it.

Well, the interview went smoothly, and then—do you think I went home? Oh, no! I hopped into the back seat of the car again; we drove to a nearby side street, where I squirmed out of my swim suit, put my luncheon clothes back on, combed my hair, fixed my face, and walked back into the Beverly Wilshire as if nothing had happened. All this took about an hour. They *had* saved my dessert (too bad it was the melting kind), but I *did* get another cup of coffee and stayed to watch all the beautiful stars modeling the garments that were to be auctioned.

In case you're wondering, yes, I did leave my underthings and hose on underneath the bathing suit, and you may be wondering also, "Why didn't she put the swim suit on underneath in the first place?" Well, it would have shown under the blouse and made my knit skirt look bumpy.

Don't you think that's a pretty racy day for a mature lady? Or for anybody? Would you do it? Hope so. I couldn't have done this if I hadn't had someone else driving the car that day, so if you're on your own, *skip* the luncheon and be sure to *always* be flexible and adapt.

Chapter 9
The Odds

The fault, dear Brutus, is not in our stars, but in
ourselves that we are underlings.
—William Shakespeare

The odds are hard to figure in commercial acting. It's like a poker game; you never know who's going to win. You are faced with the unknown over and over again. No other phase of the business is quite like this. In a play, you know which part you're going to do well in advance. You rehearse and do the same thing night after night. In a film, you get your script ahead of time, you learn it, and you do that particular character throughout the movie. Plays and films very seldom have thirty or forty people up for the same role, while in commercials, this occurs often. I have sat in interview waiting rooms with the most well known character actors and actresses of our day. Some have been series stars, movie greats, household names; and yet we're all playing the same game. Many times a complete unknown will get the role, so you have just as good a chance as anyone.

I did a regional commercial for a bank located in another state, and they were casting and shooting in California. There were three commercials involved, which required twenty-seven different characters. At the location, waiting for them to set up the lights, the director chatted with me for a few moments. He said, "We interviewed seven hundred people for these twenty-seven parts!" *Seven hundred* people! Can you *believe* it? It makes you wonder how you *ever* get a commercial. Yet, someone is going to get it—it might as well be *you*!

To beat the odds, you go to every interview available, dressed in different types of outfits, change hair-dos, attitudes, and even ages to fit the character you think they want. I have worn buns, braids, sprayed my hair gray, white, dark brown, and blond. I've dressed for weddings, funerals, golf, swimming, traveling, etc. I've been a farm wife, a wealthy widow, a grandma, a mother-in-law, an aunt, a tourist, etc., etc.—you name it. Men make similar adjustments, such as wearing various types of glasses, graying or darkening hair, adding hair pieces, mustaches and beards, and wearing different types of hats. One actor who works often always wears some kind of hat—it seems to help him get the job. The fact that he is a good actor doesn't hurt either. He has dark hair and a gray mustache, and he sprays them either darker or lighter to appear closer to the age required. Younger people need not do so much of this, but there are changes they can make to help them get a role. Wearing the correct wardrobe surely helps. Wearing a dressy suit for the role of a fisherman would be foolhardy, so every trick of the trade should be used.

At a casting session, one of my peers (a good dramatic actress, eyeing the bun on my head and the spectacles on my nose) said, "If I had to go to all that trouble, I wouldn't go to interviews." I could have retorted, "And how many commercials have you done?" But I just smiled and said, "Well, in commercials, many times your look is as important as your talent," which has been proven to me over and over.

Another actress friend about my age, pretty and blond, couldn't seem to connect in commercials. Yes, she got small parts in daytime shows and TV series, none of which paid much—but few commercials. Once we were both called for the part of an *old*, *old* lady in a commercial. I walked into the casting office and saw this very elderly woman sitting hunched up in a corner. She looked at me, and there was my friend with the best-looking old lady gray wig I've ever seen, in a dress that looked like my grandmother's. I swear I didn't *know* her at first. She had on no make-up but a thin coating of a pale beige base all over her face. She looked absolutely wonderfully old! Personally, I had never gone that far, but she went all the way. She got the job! She deserved it.

You may wonder why they didn't cast an older lady in the first place. This actress had to fly to Colorado from Los Angeles the night before the shoot, do the commercial the next day, and fly back immediately afterwards. The advertisers were afraid this might be too strenuous for a very old lady, and I'm inclined to agree with them.

The casting people usually don't know you as a person, so you must go as close to the character as you can. "What you see is what you get," is the way to present yourself. It's such a quick hurry-up business that the directors, et al, really don't have time to imagine how you'd look in another guise, so you must bring it to them.

There are approximately ninety thousand members of Screen Actors Guild, and you might ask, "How does *anyone* get a job?" It is not easy. You have to want to do it very much. You have to like the unknown, put up with irregular hours, last-minute changes of schedules, and freezing and boiling temperatures in outdoor shoots; but you'll have lots of excitement, color, and variety in your life. You may get headaches, but you will never be bored.

"Luck be a lady tonight" and "With a little bit of bloomin' *luck*" are just words from songs—and like betting on horses or baseball, a person usually loses, as you know. It has been said, "Luck is the idol of the idle." The bottom line is that you have to *work* to beat the odds. Luck is not the secret of your success; *you* are the secret of your success.

Chapter 10

Residuals, Rewards, and Many Happy Returns

Give me a heart replete with thankfulness.
—William Shakespeare

MONEY is usually the magnet that draws people to commercial acting. There was a time when famous actors were not interested in doing commercials. I can remember when they looked down their noses at them, but times have changed, as you have noticed. Bigger and better stars are now doing them, proud of it, and making thousands of dollars. Lesser-known professionals can do the same thing.

As you know, a commercial is a very short job, a few days at most. So, you are paid for the days you work, but in addition, every time it airs on television, you get paid again. You know that too, but it is important and bears repeating. In a film, you are paid once for your work, and sometimes you are on location for weeks, months, years. That's fine, but when the filming is over, so is your income. Yes, you *do* get a residual if there is a re-run of it on cable or "regular" television, but that is seldom. In a play, you will receive a salary for the time you are acting, and when the run is over, so is the money.

When I started working in commercials, my new

agent told me I was on availability for a cereal commercial, meaning, "Keep the two days open because they are almost certain to use you." Then, he admonished, "I would advise you not to make a picture deal, for you will make more money on this one commercial than you would on a six-week film job." Well, that opened my eyes to the amount of remuneration one gets for a commercial as compared to a film. Yes, I did that commercial, and my agent was *right*! The payments for that national commercial were quite large and went on for three years.

The longest run I've *ever* had on a commercial was seven years. No, it didn't run continually throughout each year, but it was money received off and on all that time for only three days work. That's hard to beat. The man who played my husband in that commercial was very upset at the time. He said he was due to start work on a film with a big star on the third day, and he wished he hadn't signed for this "dumb" commercial. You see, we were supposed to shoot for two days only, but they didn't finish and had to keep us an extra day.

I'm not aware of the stats as to the contract he had signed for the film, but I do know that they couldn't finish the commercial in time for him to get to the picture location, so they had to replace him. He was extremely angry and kept complaining and complaining! Actually, he's a very nice person, and we've been friends ever since. But at the time, he felt cheated, having missed the chance to be in this big movie. Well, it so happened that the film turned out to be a *real dud*, while the commercial ran on and on and on—for SEVEN YEARS!

Now, every time we run into each other at interviews, he looks at me, grins sheepishly, and jingles the change in his pocket. He knows and I know that the commercial made thousands of dollars for both of us in seven years and the movie would have paid him peanuts, comparatively.

Another advantage is that because the jobs are short and pay well, you have the time and the money to devote to some of your other creative activities, which is a plus. One actress I know, says, "I try to get at least two commercials a year, so that I can afford to act in a long-running play, which may pay me nothing."

*　　*　　*

A cookie commercial I was in paid residuals and holding fees, but unexpectedly, it began to snowball and began to bring surprising rewards. First, bills started arriving for dues from the American Federation of Television and Radio Artists, a union from which I'd been on withdrawal for years. Knowing that I had been doing only Screen Actors Guild work in recent years, I couldn't understand why I was receiving bills from another union. After contacting them, they told me that there was a radio commercial running, using my voice, which had been "lifted" from the cookie television commercial. This was a pleasant surprise, for I soon received additional payment for that. Shortly afterwards, my agent informed me that they were putting my picture on the back of the cookie box. This too was taken from the original commercial, paid a large sum, and I didn't even have to pose for the photo. So you can see, from a two-day job came not only the daily basic pay and residual payments, but also the radio commercial plus a "print" on the cookie box. Many happy returns!

*　　*　　*

A commercial I did for a hamburger chain was playing in eleven Southern states for twenty-one months. After that, another area bought the commercial and changed the local name and price, so I was called in to do a voice-over to quote these changes for this new market. This took exactly twenty minutes of work. The interesting thing was that my direction for the voice-over came via telephone from the Midwest to Los Angeles. This was new to me, as I don't specialize in voice-overs, and to have my director several thousand miles away, directing me by telephone, was really a novel experience! The sound engineer in the studio with me was responsible for putting it all together. Receiving payments for the original commercial plus extra payment for the voice-over made me feel very lucky and grateful.

*   *   *

Another surprise reward came in a commercial for a stock brokerage firm. Though no additional residual payments came from this, several extra days of work were the result. To begin with, two words in the script were accidentally omitted in the first days of shooting, so I was called back an extra day to add those two words. The process took about fifteen minutes, but I was paid for the whole day. This was for sound only, so there was no need to bother with wardrobe or makeup. The following day, they needed a hand shot of me pointing to a sign. They could have hired a hand model for this, but they either couldn't find a hand to match mine—or it was less trouble that way—or they were being nice to me. I prefer the last reason. This too took only fifteen or twenty minutes and paid the daily rate, so over all, it was an extremely profitable session.

You can make thousands of dollars with just one or two commercials, depending on the length of the run and whether it plays nationally, regionally, or locally. So stick with it, and you will be the recipient of these residuals, rewards, and happy returns.

*   *   *

Just when I thought this chapter about money was finished, another car commercial came along with the theme song, "Money Money Money Money," so I feel this addition is apropos. At least eleven actors were in the cast; four or five young men, two young couples, a little girl, and an older couple, so there was a part for every age group in this one. We were milling about, inspecting four or five cars, when all of a sudden, a flood of dollar bills began floating down from the sky. Immediately, we all started grabbing for the bills, and the director painstakingly shot scenes over and over to show as many of us as possible catching a dollar bill out of the air.

It is doubtful that the average viewer realizes how much care goes into choreographing a commercial like this. The bills came from a contrivance above our heads, while a compressor blew air up through a pipe shooting the money into the room. Every time they shot the bills out, the ones we didn't catch landed on the floor. There were hundreds of them and each time there was a retake, four or five members of the crew had to pick up all of them to be used in the next take. Those crew members surely earned their *real* money that day, crawling around all over the place picking up *fake* money.

This shoot went on for fourteen and a half hours. I was dancing around in high heels for at least twelve of those—twirling, twirling, twirling, grabbing for paper money.

48

Also, they wanted me to, "Walk Like An Egyptian," as the song goes, or like a duck (not certain). It was very important to them that I do this little dance correctly, for they called me back twice to make sure before they hired me. The man playing my husband had to do it too to get the job, but when they finally shot it, he didn't need to dance, just make great facial expressions and count MONEY. Though the director demonstrated exactly how he wanted the dance performed, you had to be able to keep time to the music, be light on your feet, and have good coordination. Anyway, I looked funny doing it and that's what they wanted. So do keep your body in condition for all and everything that comes up. You never know when you might be asked to walk like a duck or an Egyptian, or whatever.

The finished product was quite humorous. The close-ups on the faces of the actors as each one caught a bill were varied and unexpected. The director had pinpointed the most amusing ones. He really worked to get the best from each person, and it made the project a big success.

That car commercial with the theme song, "Money Money Money Money" in the background, paid nothing but money, money, money, money! Most car commercials are considered very special, because they usually play nationally and have extended runs. Be *especially* grateful if you land one of those.

Matt Shakman and I did two commercials together, "Grandma's Cookies" and "Wando the Magnifico Toy."

Matt Shakman

Toni Kelman/Arletta
7813 Sunset Blvd.
Los Angeles, CA 90046
(213) 851-8822

Here is Matt, a teenager in "Just the Ten of Us" and still very busy doing commercials.

Chapter 11
Kids

*You have to say what you are if you want to become what
you want to be.*
—William James

Children get a great boost in commercials. It's like the
goose that laid the golden egg for kids. You may see ten to
fifteen or more children in one thirty-second spot. It's a
wonderful way for youngsters to make enough money to
pay for their college education, or to save or invest money
for some future venture or perhaps adventure.

One must approach the jobs the same way as the
adult—getting photographs, sending them with resumés
to agents, etc. The main difference with children is that
they have an adult take them to and from the interviews
and jobs. This is a big item and one that a parent must
consider before getting involved.

In the winter, the children are called after school, so
the adult has to plan his or her days to pick up and deliver
late in the day in all kinds of traffic and weather. Too, they
sometimes have to bring their other children with them.
It takes a very dedicated person to do this. I have been on
many interviews with children involved, and it's usually
a very noisy crowded call at best. The mothers (for it is
generally the mother who is there) are so dedicated. I see
them reading to them, going over lines with them, combing

their hair, etc. The children are usually handsome and bright.

A four-year-old boy was in a frosting commercial with me, and he was the cutest, smartest child I had ever seen. Later, I said to the director, "That's the best-looking and most intelligent kid in the world!" And he said, "Why do you think he is here?" Touché. If your child is self-conscious, shy, or afraid, it would be difficult to get him into commercials. If you are really determined, and the child wants to do it very much, then, I would send him or her to a good class in commercial acting for children. Sometimes the right class can do wonders for a child and improve the youngster's self-image in many ways, not only for the profession but for his/her private life as well.

Some children, especially the very young ones, who haven't learned to be self-conscious, need no training at all. If they are happy and outgoing, a director can get them to do most anything.

As children mature, though, it is good for them to keep studying the craft of acting, reading aloud, taking more advanced classes, and doing everything possible to become the best performers they can. Do ballerinas, swimmers, skaters, pianists, ball players, singers, quit practicing? No! In almost every field, the successful person is at it every day. Why should actors be different? Yet, I have seen actors go from one interview to another without one bit of preparation beforehand. Many actors look down their noses at schools and rehearsal groups, but unless you are actually working, how can you keep up the many skills it takes to be a good actor? One must practice.

I am going to reiterate a few points here because they are important. First, the parent must be sure that the child wants to do this. Second, be certain that as a parent, you are willing to change your own schedule and run and jump at a moment's notice to drive him or her to an interview for a part he or she probably won't get. And finally, be sure that your child is outgoing with a happy personality.

Having worked with many children, I find that very few are shy and reticent. Most of them are bright, friendly, cheerful, and easy to direct. That, of course, is why they have the job.

The pictures and resumés that you send to agents should include their age, height, weight, hair and eye coloring, and what, if any training they have had. Naturally, they don't expect a tiny tot or a baby to have much of a background, so don't let that stop you if you feel you have the most adorable child in the world. Include in the child's background also, any skills the child may have, e.g., skating, skateboarding, dancing, singing, swimming, etc. Everything you can tell them about the child that would persuade the agents to sign him should be included. Send a short friendly note with a picture and resumé, asking them for an appointment for an interview. Wait at least a week before calling them, and if they like the information you have sent, they will set up an interview.

The agent usually likes to see the child, talk to him alone first, and then discuss it with the parent later. Sometimes, if the child is old enough to read, the agent will ask him to read some dialogue or a short paragraph. As with adults, if the agent likes what he sees, he will sign him. No need to go with the first agent who wants the youngster. See several agents before you make a decision. Once you have decided, you are ready to go! And I mean go!

The kid who is popular with casting directors is on the go constantly. Children may have as many as six to ten interviews per week. Of course, there are times when things are slow and you will have a respite.

At a call-back for a car commercial, we waited and waited for a little boy to get to the interview. On a call-back for a family group, they usually have picked several family units from which to choose, and they want to see them together. This little boy was to be in the group with me. His mother has two children who work often. At this time, the mother, the little girl, and I were waiting impatiently for him to show up. He was shooting another commercial about a mile away, and the director had given the mother an approximate time when the boy would be finished.

Someone else was going to drive him to our interview. It was hard on the mother and on me too, because my job was on the line. The casting director was so helpful, trying to send us all in together, since we "matched" as a family, and she was sure we would get the job. Finally the little boy came racing in, and we had the interview with the director, sponsor, and advertising people. It so happened that the little girl and I got the job, and an entirely different little boy was cast. The mother of the two children said, "I'll never understand this business—sometimes they like my daughter and sometimes they like my son—but never together!" Of course, this made it harder for her because a responsible adult has to be with the child at both the interview and the actual session. So if both of her children are working at different places at the same time, another adult has to be around to help.

When a child under eighteen is working, there is always a teacher on the set and classes are given at certain intervals during the day. The unions are very strict about taking care of children and seeing to their best interests, such as rest for the little ones and school time for the older ones.

Your agent will deduct ten percent of the young person's gross earnings before you receive the check, and all of the reconciliation sheets from the sponsor and ad agency are sent to you at the same time. This way, you will have no doubt as to working hours, deductions, fees, etc; it will all be there in front of you.

If someone wants to hire your child, and he isn't in the union, the Taft-Hartley law will allow him to work this one job without being a member. Then, he must join if he wishes to keep working. Of course, doing this one job makes him eligible for the union, which is great, because it's very difficult to get in. It is expensive too, but usually one good commercial will pay for that and then some. Most children have a marvelous time doing commercials and seem none the worse for wear for having done them. As a matter of fact, I find many of these youngsters to be more self-confident, outgoing, and cheerful than the average child. So, if you have a charming child, go for it!

"Hi," I said to a handsome little boy on the set. "What's your name?" And he said, "Jay," then added proudly, "I'm an actor!" And you know, with that confidence, he *is* an actor.

*   *   *

Practice Reading:

(Two little girls ages seven to nine dressed up in Mom's clothing and eating cereal.)

First girl: When I dress like my mom, I want to eat what grown-ups eat.

Second girl: So do I—and my mom eats Mairzy d'Oats cereal every morning for breakfast.

First girl (proudly): So does my mom.

Second girl: Isn't Mairzy d'Oats delicious?

First girl (pauses, hesitant): It won't hurt us, will it?

Second girl: 'Course not! Look how big our moms grew.

First girl (quickly): Ooh, let's eat some more—maybe we'll grow up faster (*hurriedly pouring more cereal into each bowl*).

Voice-over: Mairzy d'Oats Cereal—grow every which way but fat.

*   *   *

Practice Reading:

(Two boys eight to ten, wearing baseball uniforms and caps, sitting on a bench at a Little League park exchanging baseball cards.)

First boy: I'll trade you a Mike Scott for a Hershizer.

Second boy: Um-m-m (*looks at his cards*) Okay! (*They trade cards.*) How about a Daryl Strawberry for a Cookie Rojas?

First boy: Strawberry? Cookie? Hey, it's lunchtime! How about trading desserts? (*reaches in lunch pail*)

Second boy (pauses, makes a face—doesn't want to): Oh, well, all right, but mine is Dairyrite chocolate pudding in a cup, and yours is—

First boy (reaches in the sack): Is Dairyrite pudding too!

Second boy (still hesitant): Chocolate?

First boy (looks): Chocolate! (*boys slap hands in high fives and exclaim loudly*) All ri-i-i-ight, Dairyrite! (*They laughingly trade their identical desserts.*)

KERRI GREEN

Sometimes just an 8 x 10 glossy photograph is all that is required by the casting people and sponsors. (Sutton, Barth, & Vennari Talent Agents, 145 South Fairfax Avenue, Los Angeles, CA 90036)

Chapter 12
Teens

Lost, yesterday, somewhere between sunrise and sunset,
two golden hours, each set with sixty diamond minutes.
No reward is offered, for they are gone forever.
—Horace Mann (1796–1859)

Dear Teenagers,

There are three short words which will give you the strength and power to be triumphant in any worthwhile endeavor that you pursue.

Do you have an all-encompassing wish? Do you have a cherished hope? Do you want to succeed at something that others say is impossible? Pay no attention to any of them; follow these three powerful words. What are they? JUST DO IT!

I believe that to accomplish anything in life, these three short words can erase thoughts of failure and hopelessness and encourage you to fight on, no matter what the drawbacks.

So look ahead to your ultimate goals and JUST DO IT!

You want to do commercials? You can if you make up your mind. Being a teen, one is tempted to spend time after school hanging around malls, snack bars, or wherever kids like to hang out in your town. You can just mess around wasting time, or you can accomplish something instead. If

58

you really want to do commercials, you can follow all the advice I've given so far and hopefully realize your heart's desire. I know how difficult it is to give up a date, a television show, or a movie you want to see—but believe me, you'll be happier in the end if you go after what you want. I look back at the many wasted hours I spent in my youth, and I'm sorry about it. My grandmother used to say, "Too soon old; too late smart." Don't let the years roll by wishing, wishing, wishing, and not *doing, doing, doing*!

It is very gratifying to see so many young people doing so well today. Teenagers are more knowledgeable nowadays than when I was young—learning to work computers, to speak another language, sing, write, act, etc., accomplishing many things that adults admonished me in my youth, "Wait until you're older, then you can do it." Don't wait. Those of you who are hesitant or fearful, afraid you might make a mistake, do not be afraid—plunge in. Mistakes are sometimes the result of trying something in a different way, a creative way, your way. Emerson said, "Do the thing you fear, and the death of fear is certain." So if you stumble a little, well, didn't you learn something? You had the guts to try something new, so be proud. The more you try, the more you can perfect your idea and your craft. If you never "Do It," you never get anywhere.

You can see that the sponsors of commercials are using more teenagers all the time to brighten their spots, thereby selling more and more of their products. People like to watch healthy, happy young people swimming, skating, dancing—you name it—you are in demand.

This may sound more like a lecture than a "how to" chapter, but it will help you I'm sure. Take care of your health. In your growing years, you need lots of vitality to go to school, get to interviews, keep up your energy during a long, hard workday. You can't do it if you've been up all night the night before and look bedraggled with circles under your eyes. Make-up can't cover everything. Avoid junk foods and eat healthful, life-giving fresh fruits, grains, and vegetables. You already know all these things but perhaps never thought of them in connection with your choice of work.

There was a very pretty seventeen-year-old girl in a commercial I describe in a later chapter on stroboscope pictures. She was full of vitality, listened to the director, followed his direction, and was a joy to work with. This of course is why she's working. You girls might like to hear that she wore four or five beautiful outfits that they chose for her and was then allowed to purchase the ones she liked at half-price. Boys can do the same thing, of course. Just another incentive to keep trying.

Keep up your skills. You may be called upon to play tennis, water or snow ski, surf, skate, play an instrument, etc. The more skills you have, the more interviews you will get. This does not mean you must have all of those skills, but it is good to develop as many as possible.

Continue attending classes in acting, because more and more young people are flooding the market and the competition is getting heavier. The boys and girls who practice and study are the winners.

Follow the advice as to pictures, agents, etc., that I've written about in previous chapters, don't be afraid to try new things at interviews, be self-confident, and you will catch their attention.

Here are examples of a few ideas as to photographs for your composite:

Girls: bathing-suit pose, riding a bicycle, schoolgirl-look with books, party dress, exercise clothes, etc. If you have a special skill, be sure to include it, for you might get a call for that specific activity.

Boys might have pictures of themselves golfing, playing basketball, jogging, playing a guitar, etc. These are suggestions, of course. Whatever you can portray, have five or six different outfits and poses. This will show your versatility. If you have a great physique, show that. If you have a studious face, go further. Add horn-rimmed glasses, and wear conservative clothes. Whatever you think will sell you in the best way, use photos of those facets of your personality.

For your cover photograph (the front of your composite), have a natural picture of yourself. A smiling photo with teeth showing is the most salable. Pictures cost money, so be sure to ask around for a good photographer. Look at samples of the work, and discuss with him or her the clothes and poses that will bring out the best in you.

If you are really serious, you will use what money you have to put into the business of commercials and not throw it away foolishly. Spend your money on classes, photos, wardrobe, and traveling expenses.

Casting directors expect young people to be bright-eyed and up-beat at interviews. Self-assurance should stick out all over you, so keep an optimistic attitude, put your best foot forward, and DO IT!

Practice Reading:

(*Boy and girl sunning on the beach*)
Boy: Thirsty?
Girl: Kinda!
Boy (*Reaches into cooler*): Try this—it'll knock your socks off, that is if you had any on. (*Girl giggles*)
Girl: Sorry, I don't drink anything but diet colas. (*Pause*) What's it called?

Boy: Flirt.

Girl: Flirt? (*Sarcastically*) Suuure! (*Looks at can*)

Boy (*Persuasively*): Try it; you'll like it!

Girl: Oh, all right. (*Takes a swallow*) . . . FLIRT! (*Flirts with him*) Ooo-ooo, I *do* like it! (*Takes another long swallow*)

Voice-over: FLIRT—the soft drink with fewer calories, delicious fruity flavor, and a perfect thirst quencher.

* * *

Practice Reading:

(*Teenagers standing in line at Mexican fast food restaurant*)

First girl: Why don't we each get something different and then share, like people do in Chinese restaurants?

Second girl: Okay, I'll get Hot Sauce Harry's special— four burritos with avocado sauce.

First boy: And I'll order the four taco special.

First girl: How about a big bag of corn chips we can share?

Second boy: Great! Let's see—oh yeah—I'll get four taquitos.

(Second Scene)

(*All sitting at a table in a restaurant busily eating and sharing the various foods.*)

Second girl: Wow! This is the best way to taste all of Hot Sauce Harry's specials at one time! (*With mouths full, others nod heads in agreement.*)

Voice-over: Hot Sauce Harry's—eat Mexican, but share like Chinese.

TONYO MELENDEZ

A talented actor, spokesperson, and voiceover artist who is bilingual, Tonyo has appeared successfully in many commercials and is a living example of the rewards of study and discipline. Handsome, too, right? (Sutton, Barth, & Vennari Talent Agents, 145 South Fairfax Avenue, Los Angeles, CA 90036)

Chapter 13
In-Betweens

The great law of culture, let each become all that he was created capable of being.

—Thomas Carlyle

Dear In-betweens,

You are the most popular, most requested, most cast, and the backbone of commercial acting. You are the twenty-to-fifty-year-olds—the mothers, the dads, the neighbors, the car salesmen, the vitamin pushers, the teachers, the spokespeople, the butchers, the bakers, the candlestick makers. You get the preponderance of jobs, but you have the most competition as well. So beware, and be wise. Some of you have been acting in films and the theatre and find there is not enough money in them, so you turn to commercials. Not a bad turn to take, but be sure not to be too smug about your age category, talent, and look. You know you can do it, but you have to outshine the many others who feel the same as you. Watch commercials and see what type of person and attitude they are using for the various products. Each sponsor has its own slant as to how to sell a particular item. If you get a call for a specific product, and you have observed their commercials previously, you will have more of an idea of how they want it done.

You too must keep up your skills and perhaps learn some new ones. Why not? It's never too late.

Voice-Overs

An enormous amount of voice-overs are handled by your age group. Voice-overs, as you know, are done by people who are heard but not seen. The voices you hear constantly on commercials are done by those who are extremely adept at reading and selling vocally. These actors make a great deal of money. The bookkeepers who handle the finances in my agency say the top voice-over people can make more money than the on-camera performer. To become good at this, you must read, read, read aloud.

Read ads in magazines, read with different inflections in your voice, read with the idea of selling the product. Punch the product name; lower and raise the sound and timbre of your voice to make it interesting. Voice-overs are not as easy to do as they seem. The copy has to be read verbatim with just the right inflection, and one error requires a retake. Sponsors are extremely fussy about voice-overs and insist that they be perfect.

One actor I know, who has done hundreds of them, said that after he had read the same paragraph thirty-five times for company representatives, he finally put down the copy and said, "Sorry, fellas, I've had it! If you can't find a good one in that many takes, find someone else," and he walked out. Of course, he could afford to do that, but you can see that it's a difficult medium. Because your face doesn't show, the voice has to come over especially interesting, distinct, and clear or the listener won't understand it.

Timing too must be perfect. This is true of any commercial whether you are on camera or off. Once I had a line in a greeting-card commercial, and it ran eight seconds in rehearsal. The gal with the stop watch said, "Give it to me in seven, Gwen." One acquires a sixth sense about timing after practicing awhile, and you can almost *feel* when it is on the nose. I was lucky that time and cut it down one second on the next take. You can learn this, as with anything, with practice—just read things and time them. It isn't always rushing through a line to cut off a second or two; it's perhaps shortening the time spent on one word, or one pause, or an inflection. You can do it: it isn't too difficult.

Voice-over agent Don Pitts says, "What you do with your voice is what is important. It is up to the actor to make the copy come to life. Some of the best readers are the people who can make bad copy interesting. You may be a novice, but you may have a flair. Be yourself."

If you have been told that you have a beautiful or interesting voice, you are ahead of the game at the beginning. Work on it. Take a voice-over class to learn the basic requirements, one of which is having a three-minute tape of your voice made to distribute to agents and casting people. A good voice-over class instructor can give you the advice required for a professional tape to suit your voice and needs. Tapes are expensive, so do not have one made until you have looked into the subject thoroughly.

There are many other types of voice-overs—voices of different ages than yourself (such as babies), voices of animals, voices for animation, etc. If you are more interested in being heard but not seen, voice-overs are worth studying in depth.

Voice-over agent Rita Vennari, in the Sutton, Barth &

Vennari office, suggests reading *Word of Mouth* by Susan Blu and Mary Ann Mullin for voice-over help.

Accents

Accents may be required in voice-overs as well as on-camera commercials. On one occasion, my agent called and said I was to have a Maine accent for a commercial interview the next day. Having never done a Maine accent, I called a close friend of mine that night who helped me get in touch with a friend of hers who had an authentic Maine accent. Well, bless his heart, he called and talked to me for a while, and I practiced with him. Then, I taped his voice over the phone, so I could work on the accent later. After practicing for a while, I was sure I had it down. I didn't have the copy, so I couldn't work on that.

The next day at the interview, I boldly and bravely read my part with my newly acquired Maine accent. When I was finished, the director paused, looked at me strangely, and said, "Now read it for me without the *Southern* accent!"

Which only goes to show, better do what is comfortable for you rather than trying the unknown.

It is a good idea to have two or three accents down pat, so that you can call on them at a moment's notice. I opt for Southern, Irish, and English, because I can do those both on and off camera. Others might do Spanish, Italian, French, Japanese, etc., depending on their voice and look.

You can get records and tapes with a myriad of accents in libraries and music stores. Just listening to a recording over and over and repeating the words will help you immensely. Also there are accent and dialect coaches in many cities.

Spokespersons

Perhaps you've heard someone say that a certain actor is a spokesperson for a specific product. A spokeperson is a man or woman who usually looks directly into the camera and talks about the product. This requires a different talent than doing a scene with other actors; it's more like giving a speech in front of an audience.

Some performers are hired just for this type of work because they do it well. I'm sure you have seen the same actor many times pitching the same product because he/she is so good at selling, and naturally the sponsor will hire him/her over and over. This too takes practice.

Many car commercials have spokepersons, as do insurance companies, law firms, markets, etc. Watch the people doing them. They enunciate clearly, have an authoritative quality, and yet, they must have personality and charisma or the sales pitch will be as dull as dishwater.

For practice stand in front of a full-length mirror and read paragraphs from any publication recommending a product. Make it so interesting and persuasive that the people watching and listening will want to buy it.

"Activity is the name of the game," as my friend actress Gerry Locke says, so keep at it and you'll get the work.

Practice Reading:

Spokesperson (man or woman): Hey, guys and gals, I want to tell you about a marvelous new product called Fineshine. It's the only product you need to put shine on not only your furniture but your car as well. Even after waxing, a spray of Fineshine will make your car look brand new. As to your furniture, WOW! Fineshine makes it absolutely sparkle! Throw away all those other sprays—Fineshine outshines them all.

*   *   *

Spokesperson (man or woman): Some people say banking is boring. I say come to First Washington Bank, and you'll have a good time. We give fast service, the tellers are pleasant and well trained, our interest rates are so low you will jump for joy—we have free checking, and we always give away free cookies. So come in, have a cookie on us, and pick up a lot of knowledge about our CD's, IRAS, KEOGHS, and all those other services too hard to spell.

First Washington Bank—the good-time bank—I cannot tell a lie.

STACY KEACH, SR.

When you do TV commercials, you may get lucky, as I did, and get a famous actor like Stacy Keach, Sr., to play your husband. We were in an Amtrack together. (Don Schwartz and Associates, 8721 Sunset Boulevard, Los Angeles, CA 90069)

Chapter 14
The Nifty Over-Fifties

PRESS ON—Nothing in the world can take the place of persistence. Talent will not; nothing is more common than unsuccessful men with talent. Genius will not; unrewarded genius is almost a proverb. Education will not; the world is full of educated derelicts. Persistence and determination alone are omnipotent.
—Calvin Coolidge

Among other rewards, the beautiful part about commercial acting is that you can age and still work. You are not told at fifty-five, sixty, or sixty-five that you must retire. You are not given a gold watch and booted out the door. Other businesses do that, but not this business. If that were true, I would not be writing this book.

Some of the people who keep me going are those cute little old ladies and gentlemen I see on various commercials; some of them in their eighties and still going strong. I meet them sometimes at interviews and am amazed at their verve, vitality, ambition, and enthusiasm. I'm not sure whether it is the work that keeps them youthful, or if they are intrinsically youthful acting and thinking people. I believe it is a mixture of both. When I feel a bit depressed, I go to an interview and there is always someone there older than I am, full of vim, vigor, and good humor. Most of them drive themselves to interviews and hike from odd parking places in a no-nonsense manner full of confidence.

These people keep me going. Sometimes directors and sponsors change their minds about the age of the character they want. After I was hired to play my own age in a commercial, they changed their concept and decided they wanted a much older lady. During the session, the director kept saying to me, "Think old, Gwen, think old." If you're an actor, you can portray any age with body movement and thought—and of course, a little help from your friends in the make-up department.

Some of you more mature gals and guys who think it is all over for you in this business, take a good look around. I thought I was too old to get a decent job in the business at fifty, but I soon discovered that advertisers were hiring older people more and more to sell their products. With the aging of America, the products for the over-fifties become increasingly popular and bring in added revenue for the sponsors. Also, new products are being developed and recommended for the mature adult. You'd be surprised at the number of oldsters in show business, making more money than they ever made in their youth, because of commercials.

In ten years you can get a substantial union pension if you keep at it and have reached the required age. So look into it, get an agent, and follow all the advice I've given to the younger people—and you'll be pleased, surprised, and proud of yourselves for your accomplishments.

Keep your pictures up to date, showing any new changes in your face. No need to hide bags, wrinkles, or double chins. They want to see character in older faces, so one need not fear the aging process. Sometimes there will be a call for an old-fashioned look. Use your imagination—perhaps a touch of gray spray on your hair if needed, old spectacles, aprons, overalls, straw hats—anything that will denote a time gone by. You are not required to do this, but every little bit helps. Ask your agents questions when they call. Usually, they have very little information, but it doesn't hurt to ask. If the call is for a more contemporary look, make up and dress accordingly.

Have your pictures taken with and without glasses, your hair styled in several ways, have various wardrobe changes, and do not have the prints touched up. There is nothing casting people dislike more than to have agents send them pictures of actors looking fifty and appear at the interview looking seventy, due to having their prints touched up. So, again, keep your photos up to date.

Be sure to have an optimistic outlook when you go for the interview. Be pleasant and try to portray the character in the scene during the chitchat preceding the taping.

One needs plenty of vitality for this kind of work, so take your vitamins, eat your veggies, walk, ride a bike if possible, do some stretching and bending, get your rest, and look on the bright side.

For most people, lines get harder to learn and retain as one ages, so when you *do* get a commercial with lines, be certain to memorize them until they become second nature to you. I have known situations where they have had to shoot the scene forty times because the actor could not remember his lines. Of course this can happen at any age if one does not apply himself.

You young people who are starting in the business can look forward to a lifetime of work if you want it. There's no end to an acting career—and in the commercial field, there's more work than in films. "Success," it has been said, "comes to the person who doesn't quit too soon."

Hang in there. The Screen Actors Guild rewards you with a pension plan (as previously mentioned) that permits you to keep working and making money as long as you are able, and still receive the pension. There is also the Motion Picture Home and Hospital to care for you if you need it (one must meet the required qualifications). But until that time, PRESS ON!

*　　*　　*

Practice Reading:

Grandmother (softly, gently to camera): Hello, little baby. Do you want to be cozy and warm and feel like you're wrapped in a fluffy white cloud? That's how BABY BENTONS will make you feel! BABY BENTONS sleepers, shirts, and kimonos are all made of the softest, finest cottons.

So, baby, if you want to sleep in a fleecy white cloud, ask Mommy to get you BABY BENTONS.

(Shot of a Baby in a Crib)

Grandmother (Voice-over): Good night, sweet dreams.

*　　*　　*

Grandfather (to eight-year-old-boy sitting next to him at kitchen table, spreading peanut butter on bread): Ya know, Tommy, when I was your age, I had a peanut butter sandwich for lunch every day—sometimes with jelly—sometimes with bananas sliced on it, and sometimes just good ol' peanutty peanut butter. And you know what, Tommy?

Tommy: What, Grandpa?

Grandfather: Just like you, I still have peanut butter sandwiches for lunch, but now they call them—

Tommy (*interrupting*): YUMMY NUT sandwiches, Grandpa, because YUMMY NUT is the best peanut butter in the who-ole world!

Grandfather: Yep, YUMMY NUT! (*Takes a bite*) U-m-m-m, tastes jes' like the good ol' days!

Part II

Adventures

One of our most treasured and admired actors, Jack Klugman, in a Canon
Copier commercial with me.

Beloved actor/comedian Alan Hale, Jr., remembered especially for *Gilligan's Island*, who worked on several projects with me.

Talented actor Werner Klemperer, best known for his portrayal of Colonel Klink in *Hogan's Heroes*. A friend from my Pasadena Playhouse days.

Master of ceremonies, handsome, always-working actor Robert Wagner at one of his many philanthropic meetings. I was in a program he MC'd in Palm Springs.

Chapter 15
A Couple of Cool Capers

A smooth sea never develops a skillful sailor.
—Mac O'Grady

It looks so easy when you watch actors in commercials; the average viewer has no idea what the performer goes through to do that "easy" thing.

It was a call for a restaurant chain. The agent told me to look plain, so I did—*very* plain.

No make-up, a house dress and apron. The casting director had me do an improvisation with her for the camera. We carried on quite a sprightly neighbor-to-neighbor conversation; I, facing the camera, and she, off-camera talking to me. All the while, I was pantomiming hanging up clothes (directions in the copy). It went very well, extremely well, I thought.

When they called and told me I had the commercial, they said it would be shot in Los Angeles. Then, rain was forecast, so they changed the location to Albuquerque, New Mexico. It was the first week of December, and an outdoor shoot in Albuquerque didn't appeal to me that much.

Sometimes the communication with the actor is very sketchy. I knew they were going to fly me there on a certain day, and that was all I knew.

They never mentioned wardrobe at all, so I figured

they would furnish it at the location spot. I was sure they wouldn't expect me to carry a load of clothing on the plane.

The casting director called me at 4:30 P.M. the day before my flight and said I was to leave at 7:00 P.M. the next evening. It seemed a bit late to me, since I would undoubtedly have an early work call the next A.M.—and it would be two hours later their time, but it was not my decision.

That night at ten o'clock, a wardrobe girl called me to discuss my clothes. I was surprised. She asked me to bring three or four sweaters, three house dresses, and at least three aprons. "Okay," I said, "I'll bring them all to the production company in the morning, and you can choose what you want me to take to Albuquerque." She said, "I'm calling you from Austin, Texas." And I asked naively, "Why in the world are they sending me from L.A. and you from Austin, Texas, to go to Albuquerque?" And she said, "Honey, you're not going to Albuquerque. You're coming to Austin tomorrow, and there's no wardrobe check, it's between you and me—so bring it all with you." I thought to myself, *Well, thanks a lot!*

So-o-o, the next morning, I got up bright and early, washed and pressed wardrobe, and hauled out a suitcase in which to pack it. Incidentally, she said it was freezing there, so she'd try to get me some thermal underwear— and added that she'd bring some dresses and aprons too.

Even so, while I was getting my things together, my husband, being concerned, went out and bought some thermal underwear and some plastic see-through boots for me for warmth. "Just in case," he said.

At 10:00 A.M., the casting director called and said my plane was leaving at 5:00 P.M. instead of 7:00 P.M. *Fine,* I thought, *I'll get there earlier and still have plenty of time to get ready to go.*

At 11:30 A.M., she called and said, "We've booked you on another airline at 2:00 P.M. Can you make it?" "Oh, boy," I said to myself and started to make tracks. After rushing around, I did make it to LAX by 1:00 P.M. and was on my way to Austin.

By the time I arrived there (after an hour layover in Dallas, which is on the other side of Austin), met my ride (a young man holding a sign with the company name on it), and got to my room in the hotel, it was past 9:00 P.M. their time. No point in going to bed, because at 11:00 P.M. the wardrobe girl called and told me to bring all my wardrobe to the lobby at 6:00 A.M. the next morning. Ho hum!

After a few hours' sleep, I was picked up in the lobby, wearing a heavy coat, those plastic boots, carrying my make-up kit, an armload of clothes, and driven twenty-five miles to the location in the country.

When we arrived at the mobile dressing room, I discovered that the wardrobe girl hadn't brought one single iota of anything for me, *nothing*, no thermals, no dresses, no sweaters, no aprons, no boots, no nuthin'. She was a local girl, and evidently the production people didn't know much about her. So I wore what I brought and thanked God that my husband had bought the boots and thermals.

The wind was howling, the temperature was freezing, and there I was, standing in a large open farmyard in a thin cotton dress for over three hours! It was supposed to be spring! Ha ha! I was trying to look happy and whistle too—kinda' hard to pucker up at a time like that.

Everyone on the crew had on a heavy coat and cap and stopped every so often to warm up a bit at some heaters they had placed close by. Pity the poor actors; ah, how we do suffer. Funny how I'd rather be doing this than anything else. Well, *almost* anything. Why? The money, the challenge, and the adventure, I guess. Or am I crazy?

In retrospect, I *will* say that they were all concerned about me and put a coat over my shoulders between takes; but my teeth never did quit chattering and my nose and toes almost froze. Oops! I'm a poet.

That commercial turned out to be very popular. It had a musical score with a heavy beat that started my toes tapping the moment it came on the air. It had scenes with cowboys, and the clothes on the line looked so billowy blowing in the wind; and I looked so happy smiling and whistling away in the 32-degree "spring" air. No one would dream I was freezing in my plastic boots. Ain't "sho biz" magic?

The director surely knew how to make that one "sing!"

*　　*　　*

"Save the rain."

The very next week to the day, I was in another commercial that took twelve hours to shoot, and it was colder in Pasadena than it had been in Austin.

Twelve hours in and out of a cold stone house with no heat at all. It's a wonder I still have feet; they've been frozen so much.

The pay for that day was almost double, because one gets time and a half for the eighth to tenth hours. That warms the cockles of your heart, even if your feet are cold.

This was interesting, because we had to hurry from the house onto the porch to wave good-bye to our family leaving in a car, and it had to be raining and thundering. It was artificially done, of course, and after each shot, the director would shout, "Save the rain!" I got a kick out of that, and I'm still not sure whether he meant for the crew just to stop the rain, or to save the water. Perhaps they had just so much water to use and needed it all. Wish I had asked some questions, but I was so tired and cold by the time we finished that I never did find out how they did it. Technical crews everywhere probably know all about it. All *I* know is that it rained and thundered every time we went outside. It was wild and weird.

These experiences are nothing compared to what movie actors go through on long, long location shoots. They do things they wouldn't *dream* of doing in real life, all for the sake of the work they love.

Hope you guys don't get cold feet now and decide not to keep at it. Believe me, you'll *learn* to love it, I hope. Actually, you should really have a passion for it *all*—good or bad, to be a survivor in this business.

Chapter 16

A Frightening Trip in the Angeles National Forest

He travels fastest who travels alone [or with a stunt driver].

—Rudyard Kipling

The scariest trip I ever took was for a car commercial, which was shot in the Angeles National Forest. I was the grandmother sitting in the back seat with my two grandchildren. There was a young couple sitting in front portraying the parents.

The first day was very easy. They took hundreds of shots of us in the car—close-ups of our faces, our legs (to show how roomy the back seat was), and everything else inside and outside of the car, showing what a great vehicle it was. We drove back and forth on a very safe road, waving out the window and smiling. This took the better part of a day. In one scene, we stopped to pay our way into the park and one of the cast, portraying a forest ranger, took our money. It was a breeze. How naive can one be!

The second day was the killer! When I arrived at the location early in the morning, a van was waiting to take us to the top of a large hill. I call it a mountain! Br-r-r-r-r! It was freezing cold, rainy, and still dark up there. We actors moved from the van to the car to get warm and be ready to start. I should have guessed there was something afoot, when I saw that the two children had been replaced by two very small women, one wearing a blond wig (like the little girl's hair) and the other wearing a baseball cap to look like the little boy. The assistant director said, "Gwen, you're going to be riding with a stunt driver today." I laughed; I thought he was kidding. He *wasn't* kidding!

We started up a very slick, very wet mountain road and drove at full speed, swerving toward the edge of the cliff to pass the camera truck, then turned around on this narrow, narrow mountain road and went down again to start all over. Again and again, we'd go at full speed, it seemed, to a few inches from the camera truck and then swerve to the edge again. It was absolutely frightening! When I thought we couldn't go any faster, the director, in the camera truck, would shout through a megaphone, "Faster, faster!"

They had substituted the stunt driver for the pretend father in the car, so they used him for just the close-ups. How lucky he was! Now I could see why those short women were in the car instead of children. The law won't allow them to endanger the children. (Guess adults don't count!) The two women extras were young and spoke very little English, so I couldn't communicate with them; and they were so scrunched down in the back of the seat they couldn't see what was going on anyway. But I could. HEL-L-L-P!!!

The actor playing the father just stood around and watched most of the day, while the girl playing his wife, the two extras and I, spent seven hours going up and down that mountain road at breakneck speed. It was one of the worst days I've ever spent. Even when the driver turned the car around to go back up each time, they wouldn't let him use the turn-around areas but made him back up to the edge of the road (me in the back seat with my heart in my mouth, looking over my shoulder at a precipice).

Why? Because they were afraid that the sand and gravel on the turn-around area would get the wheels dirty. Can you *believe* it? On top of which, the stunt driver, who was marvelous but very young, started playing footsie with the girl who was acting the part of the young wife sitting next to him, and I thought, *Oh, brother, if his foot slips just once, we're goners!* Towards the end of the day, they took some close-ups of the actor playing the father and tried to have him do some of the fast driving, but he just couldn't take the chances the stunt driver took, so he got back into the car again. "Woe is me," said I.

I was very angry because I hadn't been warned about this beforehand, and when it was over, it was difficult for me to be civil to the sponsor. I could have complained to the union about it and possibly gotten more pay for this, but I thought, *Well, what's done is done, and I'm still alive, so forget it.*

It taught me a lesson, though. I will *never* take another job that could be dangerous until I've asked a lot of questions about it. Then, I can choose to do it or not. No amount of money in the world is worth risking your life over.

The topper! When the commercial finally aired, you could see the back of the car going up the hill, a close-up of a hand putting a tape in the cassette player, the actor's face for a split second, the little girl's face for a split second, my arm, my cheek, and the edge of my glasses. No smiling faces, no hand waving out the window, no little boy, no young wife showing—hardly any people at all—just the car. It was almost funny. Of course, it *was* a car commercial, and that's what they were selling. The director, bless him, was covering every possible angle to please the sponsor. He had to have a myriad of shots to cover any and every eventuality. Well, he certainly got those! And, as I've told you before, the car *was* the star.

That commercial paid a lot of money, and I'm not going to complain about *that,* but I'm warning you to ask questions when they want you to do something that might be dangerous.

The money? I EARNED IT!

Chapter 17
A Quick Journey through Time

The most impossible task you can imagine is never totally impossible.

—Anon.

I thought I had seen it all, but this commercial session for a leading battery company was the biggest one yet!

When I arrived at the first interview, the casting director said, "They are going to take hundreds of shots of you for the main holidays with a stroboscopic camera. You will be seen in at least eight holiday settings." A strobe camera can take still pictures almost as fast as a movie camera. At the interview, we had to do a short improvisation with various members of a family who hadn't seen each other for some time, hugging, kissing, and showing much animation. We carried on a short verbal exchange too, which turned out to be quite funny. It was a very happy interview.

Strangely enough, I could not put this one out of my mind; it sounded so exciting. I kept saying to myself, "Now, this is going to be a really big one, and I'm sure I'm right for it." I tried not to think about it too much, but I kept hoping I'd hear from them again. Of course, that's something I tell students never to do, as the letdown can be too disappointing if you don't get called back. Better do as I say, not as I do.

Three or four days later, the call-back came! The casting office looked almost as crowded as the first call, but when I glanced around, I noticed there were actually only five "grandmas" in contention. The rest of the room was filled with people trying out for the mom, dad, and children's roles. It was a noisy bunch, and the casting people kept coming out and "shushing" us. Finally, I went in with a group consisting of a grandfather, a mom, a dad, and three children. We were told to do a short improvised scene together, and it seemed to go quite smoothly. I was a bit apprehensive though, when I saw how tall everyone was. Evidently the powers that be decided that the grandma could be shorter, for I *did* get the part! Hoorah! It was to shoot for four days, which meant that the session fee alone would amount to well over a thousand dollars.

When the wardrobe girl called, she asked if I could bring wardrobe for Mother's Day, Easter, the Fourth of July, Christmas, New Year's Eve, graduation day, and two Thanksgivings. Wow! This was the most extensive wardrobe I've ever had to put together. I spent one whole day washing, pressing, and coordinating clothes. I won't try to list everything I took, but it was approximately twelve outfits. Those, plus jewelry and hats, made quite a car full.

As I mentioned in my chapter on wardrobe, that department brings things to supplement your clothing, so when I arrived at the production company for the wardrobe call, it looked like a bazaar in Hong Kong. The wardrobe girl had purchased around sixty outfits, including Halloween costumes for extra children coming in. She had done this on very short notice and did a marvelous job! It was a herculean task, because she then had to look at all the things we had brought and decide what we should put on to show the directors. Everything had to be approved by two directors, the one shooting all the stills and the commercial director, who was to shoot the actual commercial, which would ultimately show all the still shots whizzing by.

So, we kept running in and out of the two dressing rooms close by, where we changed. As soon as a costume was approved, it was tagged with your name and holiday, and hung on a rack. This had to be done in one afternoon, because there was only one day between this call and the shoot, and much had to be accomplished before that. Everything on television is done quickly, especially commercials. They want it good, and they want it *now,* and at times it's hard to do.

The adults came in at three and the children with mothers, fathers, or guardians came at four o'clock. By five it was like a madhouse in there. I'm not sure when they finished, but I'm certain it went on quite awhile after I left. Each actor gets paid by the hour for a wardrobe call, so it makes it all worthwhile.

They shot Halloween and the Fourth of July on the first day. They used a lot of children, and it was a great treat for them to play "dress-up" for those two holidays. They had a ball!

The second day was Mother's Day, Easter, and graduation day for the oldest daughter. They took pictures of me receiving a Mother's Day gift in one outfit, then later in another dress, I was helping color Easter eggs—then, in the afternoon, they did some shots of me with my granddaughter in her cap and gown. Of course, in every scene I was with one or two members of the family. I am not intimating in any way that I was the star of the commercial—far from it! The battery they were selling came first, then the family.

The third day they shot Christmas scenes. The photographer took hundreds of still pictures of the young family in robes and slippers opening gifts around the Christmas tree. This took the entire morning. They had purchased lovely toys and clothing for the children to unwrap. They were exceptionally kind to them and praised them often. The children were wonderful! They really worked quite hard. They smiled and hugged the members of the family and acted thrilled over each gift, even though I'm sure after a certain amount of time, they were very tired. They never complained, took direction beautifully, and endeared themselves to all of us. One little girl was only four and was a trouper all the way. At the risk of repeating myself, those of you with young children who want to do commercials, should be sure that they are good-natured, outgoing, and intelligent. They have to be or they won't get the job.

Later that day, they took shots of me stringing popcorn for the tree with the little boy playing my grandson.

The fourth day they were to shoot New Year's Eve and Thanksgiving. This turned out to be the busiest day for me.

In the morning, we did a New Year's Eve party with confetti, paper hats, noisemakers, streamers—the works! Everyone was dressed up, and there were quite a few extras there. In the midst of all the excitement, the director asked me if I could play the piano. Since I play very little, I said, "Yes, but not very well." He seemed satisfied with that, so I played a few popular tunes I had memorized years before. It was fun, for everyone was dancing to my music. Then he said, "Faster, faster," so I pounded away at breakneck speed while the dancers whirled around me. I couldn't believe I was doing this, for I hadn't played a piano in public for years. It was an added incentive for me to keep up old skills; one never knows when they will be needed—take note. Also, the director gave me a big hug after that shot, so I felt pretty good.

We finished the New Year's Eve party by lunchtime and after that, we dressed and were made up for Thanksgiving.

We were to shoot two Thanksgiving scenes. The point of the whole commercial was to show how many pictures could be taken in a year using one battery, so they were taking us from one Thanksgiving to the next.

This was the big day when they shot the actual commercial, using a different director and camera. Then, all the still photos would be incorporated into it later. Get the picture? Or should I say, "Pictures?"

In the first Thanksgiving scene, I had to carry a huge turkey on a heavy silver tray from the kitchen to the dining room. It was so heavy that two property men had to hold it for me until they said, "Action!" Then the load was all mine. The family had to come from different sides of the table to join me for the joyous Thanksgiving picture. They were all jumping over cables, getting into their correct places, trying to stay in the light, and all attempting to hit their assigned marks simultaneously. It took about ten tries, but we made it. That turkey got heavier and heavier with every shot. I discovered some muscles in my arms that I hadn't used for years and felt it the next day. In the midst of it, someone said, "What kind of a 'turkey shoot' is this, anyway?" Everyone laughed and that eased the stress and tension.

For the second Thanksgiving scene, we changed hairdos and clothes, and we actually ate some of the dinner. There were shots of us passing cranberry sauce, carrots, potatoes, etc. The adorable little girl playing my granddaughter ate an entire dinner while they were shooting. It was easy to get natural shots of her enjoying her food.

Incidentally, they had another little girl standing in for the principal child actress at different times, while she rested. Screen Actors Guild rules will let children work only a certain number of hours per day. They were using her best friend, who had the same coloring and resembled her in many ways. They were shooting her from the back, so you couldn't see her face anyway. This little girl had never been on a set before (she was not yet four years old)—so, at one point when she was standing apart from the other actors, the director, wanting her to step back into her designated spot in the scene, said, "All right now, Caroline, step in." There was no reaction from the child. "Caroline dear, step in," he said a bit impatiently. Still no reaction. Finally he said with emphasis, "Caroline—step in PLEASE!" Then in a high-pitched but very assertive lisp, she turned to him and asked, "Thtep in *what?*" So *there,* Mr. Director!

But I do digress. The still photographer took many more pictures after that, and we finally finished after four days. Watching everyone pack up and leave, was a sight to see. It's a strange and rather heart-tugging experience to leave a little pretend family and go on to another job. I noticed each child happily carrying home one of the toys used in the Christmas scene, which I thought was a nice gesture on the part of the sponsor. Every so often, more often than not, we performers run into each other at subsequent interviews or perhaps another commercial shoot, and it's like seeing dear friends again.

Believe it or not, the photographer, using a high-speed stroboscope camera, shot 7,000 photos and only 150 would be used, he told me. He added that it would take two weeks of post-production work to choose which shots would be seen.

This was the most involved commercial I've ever been in—the most wardrobe, hair, make-up, and scene changes. I wore four of my own outfits and four of theirs. This, multiplied by five principal actors plus extras, was quite a chore for the wardrobe department, which deserves a medal. My hat goes off to the property department too, which brought food for almost every holiday, Christmas trees, Thanksgiving decorations, wrapped gifts, Easter eggs, paints, etc., ad infinitum. The beautiful home where it was shot was filled with different decorations and fresh food every day for four days.

Those of you who know about films will say, "What's so special about that? This goes on all the time."

Yes, but for just thirty seconds of viewing?

Chapter 18
Overbooked, Overlooked, and Overladen

There would be no babbling brooks if there weren't stones in them.

—Anon.

You've probably heard the story or perhaps have seen the movie, *The Flight of the Phoenix*, starring Jimmy Stewart, right? Or you may have heard the song that goes, "By the time I get to Phoenix, she'll be rising," right? Well, how about, "My bungled, belated, bummer of a trip to Phoenix?" I'm *sure* you want to hear about *that*!

Two days before Christmas, a terrible time to be in an airport, but so what? I had a job to do. The job was to be in a commercial for America West Airlines at their home base, the Phoenix airport. Sounds easy, doesn't it? All I had to do was fly from Burbank, California, to the Phoenix Airport, be met by someone from the crew of the commercial production company, shoot the commercial in the airport, and fly back the next morning. No problem.

Now, let's see. Oh yes, I left my house at 3:15 P.M. to be sure to get to the Burbank airport by 4:20, an hour before my 5:20 P.M. flight out. I arrived in plenty of time, thank goodness, because the crowd and lines of people there were unbelievable! When I finally squeezed my way to the ticket counter and gave the girl my voucher, she said there was no ticket for me. "No ticket?" I asked, "but they said there would be!" She called several telephone numbers and said, "Sorry, there is no ticket for you, and we are overbooked." I went from counter to counter trying to find my ticket.

"No tickee, no flyee," I'm thinking. Come on! The stress was just beginning. It would be impossible to describe my feelings. One counter girl told me to go someplace and wait, and when she had more time, she would try to solve my problem. I walked around, I sat on my suitcase against the wall, I counted passengers, I almost cried. Finally, I went back to this really nice girl and told her I *had* to get to Phoenix. I would sit on the floor, I would sit on someone's lap, or they could sit on *my* lap. She said it was against the rules. Darn!

Finally, about ten minutes before the plane was to take off (a half hour late), she said she had called someone at the top and though they were overbooked, I could get on board. Yay!

After I was settled, the flight attendant announced that they were nine passengers overbooked and anyone who wanted five hundred dollars or a free trip to Hawaii could have one of those things if they gave up their seat. Nine guys jumped up and were out of there in a hurry. So the nine people waiting got on. Don't know *how* I got my seat.

Okay. So I'm on my way to Phoenix. Not realizing how huge the airport was before seeing it from the air. I was happy to think I would be met and guided to my destination when I landed. So-o-o-o, I disembarked (as they say) and stood in the entrance looking for a guide. Usually, on out-of-town flights, there is someone waiting for me, holding a sign that reads, something like "Commercial shoot,

America West Airlines Production Company so and so," or words to that effect. Not *this* time! No one!

Well, what did I expect? So, I went to the nearest ticket counter and asked the girl, "Could you please tell me where the airline commercial is shooting?" "What airline commercial?" she queried. "*This* airline commercial!" I answered. "Oh," she said. "Didn't know they were shooting one here." *Swell,* I thought. So, I wandered around to about five check-in counters and got the same answer every time. Now mind you, this was to be shot right in *that* airport for *them,* and no one knew anything about it.

By then, I was exhausted and almost forgot which airport I was in. I was dragging a huge garment bag, a heavy make-up case, and a bulging purse; and I'm not a very big person. Then, I spotted a man whose lapel button read, "Passenger Service." He was very helpful, said he would look into it for me, took me on a two block walk to the frequent flyers lounge, and told me to wait there until someone came for me.

By that time, it was 9:00 P.M., and I was to start shooting in make-up and wardrobe at 10:00 P.M. So far, I hadn't eaten a bite since I left home at 3:15 P.M. I was tired, hungry, and felt like going to sleep. They had coffee, cookies, and cheese and crackers in the lounge, thank goodness, or I would have starved.

At ten minutes before ten, a young woman came running in, got down on her knees before me, and apologized all over the place. They had been shooting all night every night that week and sleeping in the daytime, she explained. At 9:30 P.M., she said she sat up in bed in her hotel room and exclaimed, "My god, I forgot Gwen!" *It figures,* say I to myself. Well, to make this tale longer, off we rushed to the area where they were shooting—about a mile tram ride and voila! There they were! If I had only known sooner. Well, they were all over me, bringing me food, fitting and hemming my suit, fixing my hair and make-up—you name it! Of course, I had to run from the area where we were shooting (a regular passenger waiting area) to the ladies room to change my clothes. It was rather hectic, since there were hordes of holiday travelers all over the area watching the proceedings.

At long last, we were ready to start! It was 11:00 P.M. and I had been on my way since 3:15 P.M., plus the fact that I had been up since 6:30 A.M. packing and getting everything squared away for the trip *and* Christmas! Often I have found that wardrobe calls, travel, interviews, fittings, make-up, hair, etc., are more difficult than the work itself. When we finally started the actual work, it seemed a relief.

I was playing a lady overburdened with bundles on my way to visit my family. As I hurried toward the plane, I dropped several packages, and a flight attendant dashed over to pick them up for me. Then I had several lines to say, thanking her as we walked toward the camera. This was to demonstrate how helpful airline personnel could be to passengers. We did this over and over. In the midst of it, the director said kiddingly, "Gwen, are you drunk?" Now that I think back, I probably *was punch-drunk*; guess I was acting silly. Wouldn't you have been at this point?

After several hours, the director said, "That'll do it," and we were finished!!!!!

Oh yes, I forgot to mention that there were quite a few extras in this commercial, several of whom had been in all of the commercials they were shooting that week, which was a nice job for them. Most of them were Phoenix residents. So you see, you *can* get work in various cities.

By now, it was 2:30 A.M. I won't go into all the details, but after getting my clothes changed and my gear together, someone drove me to the hotel nearby, where I had a two-hour nap in the room of the girl who had forgotten me. At 5:00 A.M., I got my wake-up call from the hotel desk, jumped up, got myself together, met the company van in front of the hotel, and was driven back to the airport for my flight home. *This* time I had a ticket *and* a seat; you can be sure of that!

At 7:30 A.M. our time, I was back in Burbank, and I felt like kissing the ground. Guess who slept almost all day when she arrived home? It was the day before Christmas and "all through the house not a creature was stirring."

And that, kiddos, is another story in the saga of doing commercials. Do you still want to do them? Sure you do. It's a challenge, exciting, tests your mettle, and most of all, every one of them is a different ADVENTURE! Keep at it and you too can become a WEALTHY UNKNOWN in television.

Addendum: I want to assure you that the airline was not at fault in any way. That's why I felt free to identify it. It was the fault of one young girl in the production company, and you notice I didn't mention her name. Wasn't that decent of me?

Chapter 19
Two Happy Shoots

Work is much more fun than fun.

—Noel Coward

I am writing about different shoots only to show you the various types of experiences and the fun you can have as a commercial actor.

There are quite a few perks in this business, such as flying first class, the best food, receiving star treatment, etc. Nice!

The following was another car commercial, with no stunt driver needed on this one, thank goodness. Eleven of us actors, a teacher, and parents met at the Los Angeles air terminal for a trip to Portland, Oregon. Yes, it was first class all the way and a very smooth trip.

We were met in Portland by a young woman who drove us in a van fifty miles into the country to the location. Our driver was a very pretty, capable girl from Seattle. It was the first time I'd ever had a female driver. She was extremely competent and helpful. We met with members of the crew and others who had been shooting in Seattle the previous day. They were having lunch in the middle of nowhere. There was nothing around but trees and pasture and a few equipment trucks. They invited all of us to have lunch, and though we had just eaten on the plane, we managed to down some ice cream and cake. Why not? It was there. The children were having a ball running around getting rid of surplus energy, after having been confined to the plane and van for so long.

After lunch, we were driven to a pretty yellow farmhouse where the shoot was to take place and were told to wait for a decision as to when to make up and dress. They took the young married couple and the children immediately, while the man playing my husband and I sat and discussed the affairs of the world, diets, exercise, and the effects of "sho biz" on normally sane people. Then we took a long walk in that beautiful farm country. About 5:00 P.M., they said they wouldn't need the two of us until the next day. How lovely, I thought, to be paid to spend a delightful day in Oregon plus two nights in a fine hotel in Portland.

Our call wasn't until early afternoon the next day. The young adult actor in the group took the kids on a tour of Portland and the zoo in the morning. None of them had been there before, and they enjoyed it all. I read and relaxed and had a leisurely lunch in the hotel dining room.

After lunch the van picked up all of us, and we were driven back to the pretty yellow farmhouse. They didn't get to us until very late in the afternoon, but it was such heavenly weather up there that we didn't mind a bit. Finally it was our turn. The actor playing my husband and I were seated on the front porch of the farmhouse, and when the brand new car they were advertising drove up with our family in it, we stepped off the porch, went through a gate, looked over the new car, and greeted our family effusively as they got out. Actually, they had to shoot that scene only a few times, and it was finished. It didn't take more than an hour of work for the two of us. After that, they took many shots of the car and the young family getting in and out. This took several hours. It was June and they could shoot in daylight until almost 10:00

P.M. in Oregon. Unless you live in the northern part of the United States, you don't realize how late the sun sets in the summer. It was beautiful!

Not only was it cheaper to shoot in Seattle and Portland than in Los Angeles, but the added hour or so of daylight gave them extra time to perfect the shots. For that same reason, shooting in June for an October airing was extremely wise on their part.

After everything was finished, we all sat in the van, read our contracts, discussed various aspects of them, checked the hours, and signed them. One must always read one's contract very carefully. Anyone can make a mistake, and you must be sure it is all correct as to wardrobe fee, hours, travel time, double time, etc. There was a clause in them regarding video tape rights, which I didn't sign until discussing it with my agent. This was in regard to extra payment if the commercial was used in a video—say, with a movie or any other kind of show on tape. Having left it up to my agent, he negotiated later for twice the money they were offering.

That night we eventually arrived back at the hotel after ten o'clock. The dining room was about to close, but they were kind enough to stay open for us. We had a delightful relaxing dinner and a good night's sleep, before meeting in the lobby the next morning for the return trip to L.A.

You'd think we were old friends after only three days, having been together so much. We took pictures in the lobby before leaving for the airport. These pictures bring back pleasant memories.

When we reached Los Angeles, we said our fond good-byes; hoping and expecting to meet at another shoot, somewhere, sometime. Sometimes we do—sometimes we never see the actors again. And that's the way it is.

The one thing to which we look forward in anticipation is to see ourselves on the tube for hopefully, a long, long run and many residuals.

*   *   *

Everybody had a good time on this next commercial for a chicken product. We went to Patriotic Hall in downtown Los Angeles for this one. There were at least forty men there, some were actual veterans, some were actors—all of them portraying veterans of foreign wars. The director was wonderful and took shots of me dancing with the men, serving them food, joking with them, etc. I felt like I was back in the USO. Being the only female with all these men was a real *treat*! Believe me, that doesn't happen to me very often. Very often?—never! I loved every minute of it. The men had a wonderful time, ad-libbing, laughing, and enjoying the delicious chicken and accompanying side dishes that were to be seen on camera. They were all dressed in uniform and looked very authentic.

Patriotic Hall is quite an interesting building. It has eight floors and each one depicts a different conflict, with hundreds of pictures of officers and men from each foreign war. It is a very old building, filled with nostalgia, with every floor bearing and honoring the name of a prominent military hero. I cannot believe I had never been there in all the years I've lived here, so you see, commercials even give you a brief lesson in history.

In the commercial, I was portraying a very happy lady serving chicken to all of those darlin' men—and I got paid for it. It was a tough job, but *somebody* had to do it! Men in this business take note; here's a commercial where forty men worked and were paid, and only one woman. This happens often, with men portraying firemen, policemen,

107

doctors, lawyers, businessmen, car salesmen, etc. So, men, take heart if you haven't worked for a while, there's a big market for you out there. Lets face it, gals, we just have to fight harder.

In *The Flamingo Kid,* a father says to his son, "The two most important things in the world are finding out what you're good at and finding out what you like, and if you're really lucky, the two will coincide." And *I* say that being paid for it makes it perfect!

That's when you find that work *is* more fun than fun.

Chapter 20
What a Difference a Day Makes

Luck invariably favors the prepared.

—Anon.

Once upon a time, there was a television program titled, "Queen for a Day," where one lady was chosen over others to receive all kinds of attention, gifts, applause, etc.

Would you like to be Queen for a Day? It happened to me, and I'll never forget it.

I went to an interview for one of California's banks. There were only five women there that day, and we were waiting in an anteroom next to a huge sound stage. I could watch the four women ahead of me as they went through their paces. They were a hundred yards from me at least, but I could see that they were really emoting with large gestures, and much energy.

Near the camera (taping interviews) were seven or eight men and women doing various jobs, such as running the camera, directing, casting, etc., as well as sponsors and advertising personnel. I was the last one to be interviewed.

The interview seemed to go very well. They asked me to act out many things—short of standing on my head, as well as speaking the lines they had written. I had studied the lines just before the interview. When I finished, the people in charge were all smiling, which encouraged me. I couldn't understand, though, why they were interviewing such a small group for the part.

I arrived home at around four o'clock, and at six o'clock, my agent phoned and said, "Congratulations, Gwen, you got the bank commercial!" I couldn't believe my ears. No waiting? No call-back? It *was* surprising.

Soon afterwards, I discovered that they had been looking at women all week, and I was the last one to walk in the door and the *one hundred and fortieth* person to be interviewed for the job! They told me later that the moment I walked in, there was a unanimous sigh of relief, and they said, "There she is!"

Now, before you get the idea that I think I'm God's gift to the television industry, remember what I said in previous chapters; in essence, that in commercials, the *look* comes first, then the personality, then the talent and know-how. Upon viewing the story-board, I could see that I looked very much like that woman in the picture, so I felt very blessed.

The shoot for this commercial was on a Sunday, so they could utilize the bank. One gets double pay on Sunday, so the actor is not going to complain about that! Right?

At 7:00 A.M. they were shooting me in front of a small house, leaving for the bank. I said my first line and smiled at the camera crew, as I walked down the steps to my destination.

This was supposed to be a home movie of Mrs. Pearsall going to the bank. The next location was a shot of me waving in front of the bank, with the remainder of the shots inside, as I walked around the building, waving and talking to the tellers, bankers, etc.

The point of the commercial was to show how much

more attention customers get from a small bank, as compared to a large one.

This thirty-second commercial took nine hours to shoot, with a half-hour off for lunch. Having to change locations many times for many scenes, both inside and out, took a great deal of time. Cameras, lights, and equipment, all had to be moved. So you can see why it took nine hours, and I was running around in high heels all the time. It wasn't their fault; the shoes matched my outfit, and that's the way I like it. Okay?

This was the first time I ever felt like a queen. There were at least fifty people there—the director, the sponsors, the assistant director, the bank employees, the camera crew, sound men, extras . . . you name it.

All day everyone treated me like I was something special. Some of the women watched closely every move I made, on and off the set. I began to feel rather self-conscious, but it was exciting to get all that attention.

They say that everyone gets at least fifteen minutes of glory in a lifetime, and this was a whole day. I loved every minute of it.

That commercial ran four or five times a day for months. Everywhere I went, someone stopped me to say, "Hi, Mrs. Pearsall," and then laughingly tell me how much they enjoyed it, because it really was a funny character I was playing. Many friends called on the phone, saying it was the best thing they had ever seen me do. These kind responses made me feel humble.

Actually I give all the credit to the wonderful director, who praised and encouraged me to be better than I thought I could. His name is Philip Labhart.

Yes, I know this is only a thirty-second spot, but it's often harder to make an impact in a short time than in a long scene.

Despite the fact that your look is most important, you still must practice your reading and memorizing skills. Stick to your goals. Keep at it, and you too can be made to feel like a King or Queen for a Day, or hopefully, many days.

Russell Baker, the host for Masterpiece Theatre, says, in essence, that if you're not on TV in America, you're not part of American culture. He may have said that with tongue in cheek—even so, everyone seems to want to get into the act.

I do hope *you* decide to get into the act SOON!

All the patience, hard work, persistence, study, and fruitless trips to interviews seem negligible when one is rewarded with one glorious memorable day like that and the prospect of many more in the future; and, lest we forget, there's always that beautiful residual check!

What a wonderful business!

*   *   *

THE HEIGHTS BY GREAT MEN REACHED AND KEPT
WERE NOT OBTAINED BY SUDDEN FLIGHT,
BUT THEY, WHILE THEIR COMPANIONS SLEPT
WERE TOILING UPWARD IN THE NIGHT.
                                        —Henry W. Longfellow

Chapter 21
Wrapping It Up
(12 Steps)

Lines to remember:

1. Be early for appointments.
2. Be upbeat at auditions—smile—make them like you.
3. Be prepared—be self-confident when you audition.
4. Think as if you're going to get the job.
5. When you read the copy (unless otherwise directed), read it as naturally as if you're talking to your best friend or neighbor.
6. When there is more than one person in the commercial, listen carefully to what he or she is saying and react accordingly.
7. Go to every *interview*—be glad they are sending you. Many actors would be thrilled to go in your place.
8. When you have a job, do what the director tells you—don't argue.
9. Keep your car in good condition. It's no fun to be stalled on a canyon road or freeway going to or from work.
10. Stay away from alcohol, drugs and cigarettes. Your career will be in jeopardy otherwise.
11. Have a passion for the thing you want to do, and then

fall in love with what you are doing. Focus your attention on *that*!!!

12. Overcome rejection and disappointment by going on to try again—then you are heading for success.

GO FOR IT!

And that, kids, is a wrap!

Extra Added Attractions

I have found that writing thank-you notes is a thoughtful thing to do—not expected and not required, but thoughtful. I've included only two as examples. These were the actual ones I sent; one is to a director and one to a casting director.

Dear Mr. Yarbrough,

Thank you so much for all your efforts in my behalf—for choosing me and for being so pleasant during that cold, windy shoot in Texas. The logistics must have been extremely difficult under those conditions, but you made it all work.

A friend called me from Elkhart, Indiana, last night and said he had seen the "Long John Silver" several times and *loved* it!

Hoping that you continue to be the successful director you are and thanking you again, I am

Yours very sincerely,

* * *

Dear Debby,

Thanks so much for having me in to read for the C. &

P. Telephone commercial. It turned out to be a sixty-second spot with several attractive scenes. I'm only sorry it won't be shown here. It seems most of my best work is scattered somewhere in the great Midwest and East—Murphy's law, you know.

Wishing you continued success in your chosen field and thanking you again, I am

Yours sincerely,

As I said, this is not necessary, but I do it because I am truly grateful; and it does make for pleasant relationships.

* * *

Suggestions for a few schools and workshops familiar to me in Los Angeles:

Tony Barr's Film Actors Workshop—5004 Vineland Avenue, North Hollywood CA 91601. An intensive course in film and television acting for more advanced students. (818) 766–5108.

Everywoman's Village—5650 Sepulveda Boulevard, Van Nuys, CA 91411. Call for a brochure (818) 787–5100, (213) 873–4406. Acting in commercials for both women AND men. Affordable—in a relaxed environment. Good for beginners.

Kathleen Freeman Enterprises Studios—11026 Ventura Boulevard, Studio City, CA (818) 761–5181. On-camera workshops, film comedy acting—free audits.

Geo Hartley Workshop—5110 Los Feliz Boulevard, Hollywood, CA 90038 (213) 662–9661

David Lehman—1819 West Verdugo Avenue, Burbank CA 91506. (818) 845–1549. Film acting coach, scene study—a great help in preparing for any commercial acting.

The Stockwell Studio—10500 Magnolia Boulevard, North Hollywood CA 91601. (818) 761–8240. Acting on camera taught by Guy Stockwell, well known name in film and TV.

Tepper-Gallegos, Inc.—7033 Sunset Boulevard, Suite 208, Los Angeles CA 90028. (213) 469–3577. A very professional workshop for children and adults. They do casting also.

Weist-Barron-Hill—4300 West Magnolia Boulevard, Burbank CA 91505. (818) 846-5595, (818) 880–5141. Classes taught by Lyle and Andrea Hill, a talented couple. They have guest directors, casting directors, and are reasonably priced. Weist-Barron has five branches across the USA.

Remember the colleges:

Loyola University, U.C.L.A., U.S.C., California State University Northridge, Los Angeles Valley College, Los Angeles City College—these are schools I have audited. Check your local brochures for information about classes in your area.

*   *   *

One of the best sources for help is *Drama-Logue* magazine, which comes out every Wednesday on the newsstands. It has information regarding the stage, screen, television, radio, schools, workshops, photographers, reading, reviews, previews, etc. These are mostly about happenings in Los Angeles, New York City, San Francisco, and San Diego—but helpful wherever you live.

I would suggest getting a subscription to this:

116

DRAMA-LOGUE P.O. Box 38771
Los Angeles, CA 90038–0771

*   *   *

If you are from out of town and want a good place to stay while trying to get your child into commercials, you can rent an apartment by the week or month at the Oakwood Apartments. The address is 3600 Barham Boulevard, Los Angeles, California 90068; (213) 851–3450. The Oakwood caters to people with kids trying to get into the business. It has bulletin boards featuring articles as to interviews, agents, upcoming readings, etc. Plus, a camaraderie develops with the people there, sharing their news and views about the commercial scene. It gives you a chance to look around and consider various options before you make long-range plans, and you will not feel alone in a strange environment.

*   *   *

An enterprising mother, Barbara Schiffman, founded an organization in 1988 called the Hollywood Screen Parents Association. This association helps parents of child actors, or those who aspire to be, to obtain information about the entertainment industry.

There is a nominal one-time registration fee for membership. A free registration kit is sent on request with resource lists and tip sheets for show business newcomers and families of working young actors.

Membership is thirty dollars per year, and members

117

receive newsletters and pamphlets advising them as to classes and all phases of the business.

Write to: Screen Parents Association
4720 North Vineland Ave. #235
North Hollywood, CA 91602
Phone (818) 955-6510

Glossary

Words in this book and others you may read or hear at interviews and work situations.

A.D. Assistant director.

Ad lib. To improvise lines or a speech.

Agent. The person who sends you to interviews.

ASAP. As soon as possible.

Call-back. When you are asked to come back for another reading for the same part: an encouraging sign.

Casting director. The person who gets you into the casting office to be interviewed for the job—hoping you will be hired.

Cold reading. Reading copy for the first time after a few minutes study or none at all at an audition.

Composite. A group of photographs of yourself (sometimes with a resumé) on one sheet.

Copy. The script; the words you say in a commercial.

Cu. Camera close-up.

Cue cards. Large poster-size sheets beside the camera with the copy printed for you to read.

EXT. Exterior or outside camera shot.

Glossies. Shiny eight by ten photos.

Head shot. Photograph of just your face and head.

INT. Interior camera shot in a house or building.

Interview. A face to face meeting with a person who is to examine you as to your qualifications for the job.

Location. Where the shoot takes place.

LS. Long shot; where the subject is far from the camera.

The Mark. A tape on the floor where you stand to perform.

MCU. Medium close up. (Camera)

Monologue. A dramatic or humorous speech by one actor.

POV. Point of view.

Promo. A commercial usually promoting a service.

Residuals. Money received for every time the commercial airs after the original session fee is paid.

Resumé. The history of your background of work in show business.

SASE. Self-addressed, stamped envelope.

Scale. Basic union pay for a commercial.

Session. The day/days the commercial is shot.

The Shoot. The photographing of the commercial.

Sign-in sheet. What you fill out before your interview, e.g., name, size, age, etc.

Slate. State your name and sometimes your agent before you perform in the commercial.

Sotto. Softly.

Story-board. Pictures of the commercial. Sometimes it looks like a comic strip.

Stroboscope Camera. Takes still pictures almost as fast as a movie camera (Dictionary definition is too technical).

VO. Voice-over.

WS. Wide shot (Camera).

Wardrobe. What you wear in the commercial.

A Wrap. It's finished. Th-th-th-at's all, folks!

About the Author

Gwen Horn Willson gives much credit to the Pasadena Playhouse School of the Theatre for her start in show business, subsequently appearing in over fifty plays in California and the Chicago area. As a singer, she was featured at the Ambassador West, Drake, and Edgewater Beach Hotels in Chicago and traveled extensively with the USO. For many years she performed in a one-woman show, utilizing her various talents as a stand-up comedienne, actress, singer, dancer, and songwriter.

Gwen has appeared on TV and radio as a talk-show hostess and actress, plus acting in films.

Having done over one hundred commercials, they soon occupied most of her time. Many have been showing continuously in the U.S., Canada, England, and Mexico for the past dozen years.

Recently, she has conducted classes for aspiring actors to help them get started in the commercial field.

Gwen is a member of the Pasadena Playhouse alumni Association, Pacific Pioneer Broadcasters, The Masquers Club, the DOLLS, Inc., Screen Smart Set (Motion Picture and Television Fund Auxiliary), The MacDowell League, The Southern California Motion Picture Council, People Helping People, Screen Actors Guild, and the American Federation of Television and Radio Artists.

Gwen Willson—Some of the TV Commercials done in the '80s and '90s

FOX PHOTO, with George Gobel
IRS, with Cesar Romero
HERTZ RENT-CAR, with O. J. Simpson
AUNT JEMIMA PANCAKES
FTD FLORIST
McDONALD'S McNUGGETS
WET ONES, for British TV market
ALLSTATE INSURANCE
CHRYSLER K-CARS, for U.S. and Canada
NORWEST BANK
BOB'S BIG BOY— (Shoney's Salad Bar)
OSCAR MAYER BOLOGNA
NATIONAL HOME LIFE INSURANCE, with Art Linkletter
DISNEYLAND
HOT SHOT BUG SPRAY
LONG JOHN SILVER RESTAURANTS
MAYTAG, with Jesse White

C & P TELEPHONE COMPANY
FOX PHOTO, #2
MIDAS MUFFLERS
RCA TELEVISION
NISSAN CARS
HALLMARK CHRISTMAS WRAP
HYDROGENE OF JAPAN
COLDWELL BANKER
GETTLEMAN BEER (Miller Brewing Company)
BETTY CROCKER FROSTING MIX
MULTI-MEDIA (Medical Industrial)
MATTEL TOYS DOLL HOUSE
DODGE DYNASTY CAR
KELLOGG'S RICE KRISPIES
ENERGIZER BATTERIES
AMTRAK, with Stacey Keach, Sr.
WANDO THE MAGNIFICO—toy
FRITO-LAY, Grandma's Cookie Snacks; plus

radio commercials &
picture on box
AMERICAN ELECTRIC
POWER
BOB'S BIG BOY,
additional voice-over for
expanded coverage
WEYERHAUSER
LUMBER
COLDWELL BANKER 2
CARL'S, JR.
NEW ENGLAND
TELEPHONE—two
different commercials
TYSON CHICKEN
KABC PROMO
NABISCO COOKIES
FOSTER FARMS
CHICKEN
EDISON ELECTRIC
PIPER, JAFFRAY &
HOPWOOD—(Stock
brokerage firm)

INTERNATIONAL
HOUSE OF PANCAKES
KRAFT MIRACLE WHIP
SALAD DRESSING
GENERAL ELECTRIC
CREDIT CARD
CREDIT UNION
ASSOCIATION OF
NORTH AMERICA
CALIFORNIA SAVINGS
BANK
KABC NETWORK
PROMO—2
DORITOS
CRISPY-LIGHTS CHIPS
CANON COPIER, with
Jack Klugman
THE NEON ARMADILLO
BUENA VISTA
PICTURES
SOUTHERN
CALIFORNIA SAVINGS